# Career Journeys for Young People

## A starter guide for parents and carers

Written by the Careers Writers Association

Bookcareers Publishing

## Career Journeys for Young People:
### a starter guide for parents and carers

### Publisher's Note

Every possible effort has been made to ensure that the information contained in this book is accurate at the time of going to press, and the publishers and authors cannot accept responsibility for any errors or omissions, however caused.

Neither the authors nor the publisher take responsibility for any consequences of any decision made as a result of information contained in this book. When seeking career guidance, always choose a Registered Career Guidance Professional from the Career Development Institute.

First Published in Great Britain 2019
by Bookcareers Publishing, an imprint of bookcareers.com
10 9 8 7 6 5 4 3 2 1

© Careers Writers Association 2019
Illustrations © Chris Targett 2019

The moral rights of the authors have been asserted.

ISBN (print)   978-1-9996109-3-7
ISBN (eBook) 978-1-9996109-4-4

Typesetting by Andy Southan of Big Pond Design

# Contents

Introduction – Steve Stewart OBE

## At school
1. Career ideas for 11-13 year-olds: how to start introducing them – Jill Valentine — 01
2. GCSEs: what they are and how to do well – Paul Greer — 11
3. Years 10 and 11: career planning and choices – Alison Dixon — 21
4. Year 12: looking forward – Mark Yates — 29

## Moving on
5. Further education: why consider it? – Mark Yates — 37
6. Apprenticeships explained – Cerys Evans — 45
7. UCAS personal statements: what are universities really looking for? – Alan Bullock — 57
8. Clearing made clear – Gill Sharp — 67
9. First year at university: surviving, thriving and growing a career – Gill Sharp — 77
10. Life's opportunities: how to make the most of them – Debbie Steel — 87

## Entering the real world of work
11. The labour market: keeping up with the changes – Michael Spayne — 95
12. The labour market: how to find the best information for you – Helen Janota — 105
13. Application forms made simple – Ellie Stevenson — 115
14. Work experience: how to make the most of it – Susanne Christian — 125

## Back-up and support
15. 'What happens if it all goes wrong?' A philosophy for careers – Chris Targett — 135
16. Career myth busting: common career misconceptions – Elaine Mead — 143
17. Useful websites to explore – Hilary Nickell — 151

You will also find useful websites at the end of most of the chapters in this book.

# Introduction

The 21st century is an exciting time to be growing up, with all sorts of opportunities and possibilities open to youngsters as they go through secondary education, and particularly when they are deciding whether to enter employment or training or continue their studies.

However, the worlds of work and education are changing so rapidly that it is often difficult for those not in the know to keep pace. Those leaving school, college or university today will most likely have several different careers – some of them in areas that are only just emerging or maybe not yet dreamed of. This means that it is even more important not to leave occupational choices to chance. So I am delighted to introduce this book by the Careers Writers Association which will be of enormous help to parents and other carers looking to support young people through the often complicated options that will lead to their future.

There are many materials aimed at teenagers, but very little that is specifically targeted at the people, like you, who are most concerned with their well-being. In addition, much of what is already out there focuses on just one age group or theme, rather than looking at the whole careers journey, not to mention some of the crossroads, barriers and navigational dilemmas that can crop up en route. This guide gives a much needed 360 degree view of the whole process, identifies key issues and demystifies each stage.

Whatever the age or aspirations of your child or children, you will be able to find information, explanations and solutions that will help you to help them. It is all in here: from just starting out at secondary school and tentatively exploring job ideas right through to beginning employment or moving to further and higher education. The authors are all well-established careers writers, most of them also specialist careers advisers, so they speak from experience of interacting with a range of clients and understanding what matters to them and their families.

As Chief Executive of Careers England I have spent my own working life enabling young people to move forward with their lives. I am also a parent myself, so I fully appreciate how this book meets your needs and answers your questions. I cannot recommend it too highly, wherever you are based in the UK or the international community. Use it to give those you love the best possible head start.

*Steve Stewart OBE*

## Acknowledgements

In memory of Alan Whicheloe
1935-2019

With thanks to our authors:

Alan Bullock, Alison Dixon, Cerys Evans, Chris Targett, Debbie Steel, Elaine Mead, Ellie Stevenson, Gill Sharp, Helen Janota, Hilary Nickell, Jill Valentine, Mark Yates, Michael Spayne, Paul Greer and Susanne Christian.

Special thanks to Chris Targett for the illustrations.

You can find out more about us by visiting our website
www.parentalguidance.org.uk

# Chapter 1

# Career ideas for 11-13 year olds: how to start introducing them

*Jill Valentine*

The aim of this chapter is to provide you with ideas and helpful tips on how to introduce the notion of career ideas to your 11 to 13-year-olds. To do this, I have divided the chapter into the following sections:

- getting into their world
- the why, when, how, where and what of introducing 11 to 13-year-olds to careers ideas
- 10 top tips
- useful websites.

You will also find quotes from parents, young people and advisers to inspire you.

*'Looking for a job is a long way off so it doesn't really matter at the moment. However, I have had chats with a friend about set design and we looked on the internet but it was confusing, so we gave up.'* Eva, aged 12

## Getting into their world

For any young person between the ages of 11 and 13, there is a lot going on in their world – starting secondary school and adapting to the changes this brings, starting to make the initial changes into adulthood, and setting out on their journey of discovery, new things, new people and new ideas.

The chances are, with all this going on, their attention is not likely to be drawn towards a future career. And who can blame them?

The range of careers that young people know about is often limited. When asked 'What jobs do you know about?' nine times out of ten the responses will include: teacher, vet, police officer, nurse, doctor, dentist and firefighter. And why should we be surprised? These are the people they will have come across in their lives.

*'I want to be an RAF Pilot when I am older.'* Elliot, aged 13

Your 11 to 13-year-old may have fixed ideas about what they want to do and these plans may be grand or on the contrary quite modest, *'I want to be Prime Minster'*, *'I just want to be happy and have enough money to live'*. These might be the career plans for this week but as you know they could be very different next week.

To help them on their journey you could begin by really taking note of the things that they are interested in or what captures their imagination. What type of books are they reading? What TV programmes do they like? Who do they follow on social media? What are their favourite subjects at school? This will be your hook to start introducing career ideas.

*'I never had careers advice at school myself and therefore I would never have considered the need to raise and discuss different possibilities with my children.'* Sarah, writer and parent

## Why should you start introducing career ideas to 11 to 13-year olds?

In all likelihood you are reading this chapter as you are all too aware of the wide range of careers available and don't know where to start. So, I think, the common sense answer to the question 'Why should you start...?' is, it is never too early to start and it will certainly help with any choices faced in the future.

For example, in most schools GCSE choices need to be made in year 8 or 9. Whatever the choices made at this stage, and whatever the results eventually gained, they will inevitably have a significant impact on the A levels that your child will be able to go on to study.

At this stage the key message is there are a lot of different career paths which at first glance may appear overwhelming, but at this stage your son or daughter should not be feeling under pressure to decide which one to take.

That being said, there is absolutely no harm in opening up discussions around different jobs, and in what way they differ, and researching routes into some of these.

## When should you start introducing career ideas to 11 to 13-year-olds?

The short answer is when they are ready. Some may argue that girls may want to discuss career ideas perhaps a bit earlier than boys. A lot can change between the ages of 11 and 13. In these two years they may become engaged, but don't assume this. There is little or no point in talking to, or trying to engage with, your son or daughter about careers if they are not interested. To quote my son aged 13, *'Mum I am so not interested'*, at which point, he promptly changed the subject.

You will know, if your child wants to continue the discussion or if it makes more sense to postpone the discussion for another six to 12 months.

## How should you start introducing career ideas to 11 to 13-year-olds?

An obvious way to begin is by **hooking into their favourite school subject/s** and this can be a great starting point for further research.

So if Spanish is a subject they enjoy, you could explore what jobs use a modern language. I think with this example, all of us would need support in seeing beyond the obvious translator or Spanish teacher. However, with further research you might have captured their imagination with the role of an international aid development worker or a distribution manager. For details see Prospects website, listed at the end of this chapter.

> *'I think television provides a very useful initial exposure to a wide range of jobs. There are some great nature programmes etc. which can be a good way of sparking off ideas.'* Phil, secondary school teacher and parent

Another approach is by looking at **their interests outside school**. Let's say, for example, they are interested in running. The next stage might be to start exploring why this is important to them. *'Why do I like running? I don't know – I just do. No, I know why, because I can get away from the cars etc. I just love all the open spaces. It makes me feel good running on my own'.*
The conversation might twist and turn and **ideas may start to emerge** for example: a love of the countryside, exploring, keeping fit, feeling free, being in charge, reading maps etc.

By digging deeper, you are giving them the space to begin to articulate in their language what **really matters to them**. This short extract above is full of golden nuggets revealing preferences.

> *'Career exploration at this age is about finding out what you enjoy and where your strengths lie, rather than on deciding on a career direction.'* Cerys Evans, careers adviser at a secondary school

This type of discussion could be the start of a journey to uncover their values, priorities and passions and may, in some cases, take many years. It is easier, and will certainly take the pressure off you and your child, if you both see it as a journey of discovery.

At a later date, building on the example above you might say something like: *'I have found a website on environmental jobs/an opportunity to do half a day of dry stone wall building with the National Trust/a TV programme on the rapid ice melt in Greenland'*. You can start to build on these ideas but be patient – it is likely that you won't 'get it right' first time, but at least you might start to plant some ideas.

The more activities or clubs young people are involved in, the more exposure they will have to developing employability skills, and understanding different career sectors – and knowledge of the variety of roles which fall in each of these sectors. Obviously cost will be a factor in how many and which clubs or activities your child is able to join but, if you are lucky enough to be able to afford even just one outside activity for your child, there will be definite positive results from this.

*'With students, regardless of their age, if they are unsure about what career to consider, I try to get them to imagine what their friends might say are their skills, however big or small these might be. This is often a good starting point, particularly with those who find it hard to talk about themselves.'* Jill Valentine, employability adviser at a university

Let's look for example at the benefits of being involved in a swimming club. This activity alone would be beneficial to your child as it would provide an opportunity for them to increase their fitness, stamina and expertise in swimming and would also provide them with an undeniably invaluable life skill. However, in addition to these skills, membership will also contribute considerably to their team working, independence, communication, resilience and, above all, commitment skills. These developed skills are vital and are now termed 'employability skills' as they are considered fundamental to almost all roles within almost all job sectors.

Another method to help expand their knowledge about jobs roles is to do a **job association game**. An easy example to start with, is to ask them to think of the different jobs that exist within their school. They might begin with a teacher, but soon be able to branch out and see different roles including SENCO teacher, head of year, head of department, librarian, mentor, counsellor, careers adviser, receptionist, OFSTED inspector, lunchtime supervisor, after school leader etc.

You could then, if you wish, broaden this exercise by talking about other places of learning i.e. nurseries, pre-schools, further education colleges, sixth form colleges, universities etc. Quickly they will see the vast array of jobs associated with education.

Another suggestion is to brainstorm roles within an institution or workplace, e.g. hospital, law court, sports centre, laboratory, shop, restaurant etc. In my experience this type of activity works more effectively if you have recently visited these places or are planning to do so. This will help your child to visualise the different roles within that setting.

*'On a scale of 1-10 where 10 is very interested, how interested are you in jobs for yourself in the future?' '4/10.'* Anna, aged 11

## Where should you start introducing career ideas to 11 to 13-year-olds?

This might seem like a strange question to ask but is actually an important consideration.

The answer to this is probably '**anywhere**', **except** when sitting at a table at home with a computer or during a meal. You want this to be a light-hearted discussion where there is no pressure and no right or wrong answers to be had. The most effective time to start discussing ideas is ideally when your child begins to ask questions out of curiosity.

If you come across someone during the day who you think has an interesting job make a point of using them as an example. On the radio you often hearing people being interviewed who have less obvious jobs. I remember an interview with a buyer of beds for John Lewis – a job based around testing the comfort of mattresses. More recently there was a programme focusing on a job as a snowboarding instructor outlining what this involves.

When you are out and about, particularly in new places, why not think about the people working around you and if appropriate, ask them how they got into their role. On the whole people are more than happy to talk about their jobs and the routes into the position.

---

*'At school I find that posters are a great visual tool. I get them to think about their favourite subject as a starting point and then encourage them to think and add career ideas around it; this format is similar to a mind map.'* Rebecca Taylor, careers adviser at a secondary school

---

## What career ideas should you introduce to 11 to 13-year-olds?

As a parent or carer you can introduce career ideas to your 11- to 13-year-old, but please do not, and ever feel you need to, take on the role of the careers adviser. Throughout this publication we have provided what we consider to be relevant and useful websites, to help you on your way. If your child still needs support it might be useful to encourage them to make an appointment with their school careers adviser, if there is one, or with the teacher within the school who is responsible for career decisions.

Working out what you want to do is hard and might be something that needs to be considered more than once. We are now living in a society where the average worker currently holds ten different jobs before the age of 40, and this number is projected to grow.

So, all we as parents or carers can realistically do is be there to support and advise as far as we are able. We can do this most effectively if we are open and ready to listen and to talk through ideas, however weird and wonderful they might at first appear, at a time and a place that suits your child.

---

*Students can be challenged to think about their best two/three subject and then to try and think of careers that involve all these subjects – this challenges students to think about what a job actually involves and how it might then link to subjects.'* Rebecca Taylor, careers adviser at a secondary school

---

# 10 top tips for introducing career ideas to 11 to 13-year-olds

1. **Do not force it** – if they are not interested in discussing careers, do not push ideas on to them. It will only put them off.
2. Encourage them to develop their interests in whatever they fancy, by undertaking **further research** looking at **related books, websites, articles, YouTube videos, films, TV programmes** etc.
3. If they are interested in a particular area, you might be able to buy them a second-hand **game or activity to get them started.**
4. Encourage them to do **extra-curricular activities** outside school as this builds up confidence and starts to build upon their skills.
5. Help your child to start to think about their **strengths and weaknesses**. If they do something particularly well, let them know about it.
6. If you are working, talk to them about your job. **Tell them what you like and dislike about the job.** This will help them to get a realistic picture of work. In most cases, sadly, the 'perfect job' does not exist.
7. If you can, although it is not always easy, why not think about **taking your child to see where you work** – perhaps in the school holidays. It could just be for a couple of hours, to give them a flavour of the job.
8. If your child is ready, you may want to encourage them to think about a **part-time job** e.g. delivering a local magazine, papers or leaflets. (N.B. There are restrictions on the hours and type of work someone under school leaving age may do – check with your local authority.)
9. If the school your child attends offers **work experience** at the end of year 10, you could use this **as a hook to** start discussions and as an opportunity to try out a particular job or working in a particular environment.
10. Remember, if they don't yet have career ideas, the **first step** is to find out what they are interested in.

*'I think it is difficult to make a decision at this age. The choices need to be broad enough to ensure they have the flexibility to go into something else, should they change their mind.'* Emma, parent

## Useful websites

Find out what you like and what you could do:
www.icould.com/buzz

Career ideas with science and maths:
www.futuremorph.org/11-13/

See the Informed Choices publication on making decisions about post-16 choices and information on pre-16 qualifications and university entry:
www.informedchoices.ac.uk

Gameplan is a free games-based website provided by King's College London that allows 10 to 14-year-olds and their parents to explore university:
www.gameplan.ac.uk

The website for graduates but invaluable for everyone:
www.prospects.ac.uk

Initiatives:
www.employeesmatter.co.uk/bring-your-child-to-work-day

Jobs for 11-year-olds:
www.thebalancecareers.com/jobs-for-11-year-olds-2085431

Future jobs:
www.kent.ac.uk/careers/Choosing/future-jobs.htm

**Chapter 2**

# GCSEs: what they are and how to do well

*Paul Greer*

The aim of this chapter is to provide an introduction to GCSEs, explaining how they came about, and highlighting the most significant changes and developments. It describes both compulsory and optional subjects, and the importance of each to academic and vocational progression, and to career choice. It identifies useful 'dos' and 'don'ts' for candidates, and how schools and colleges can help by providing information, encouraging or supervising exam preparation, and ensuring students with special needs are not disadvantaged. The change from a letter to a numerical grade scale is described, and the need for high achievement for certain options is addressed.

## What are GCSEs?

The letters GCSE stand for General Certificate of Secondary Education, an academic qualification taken by secondary-level students in England and Wales. It was introduced in 1988 to provide a single system and range of grades to replace the dual one represented by O (Ordinary) levels and CSE (Certificate of Secondary Education). Its aim was twofold – to simplify grading through a single letter scale (of A-G) replacing two separate numerical ones, and to open the full range of grades to all students, something previously not possible. In the 30 years since, there have, hardly surprisingly, been many changes; these include the range of subjects offered, syllabus content, exam format, methods of assessment, and even the grades themselves – A* being added in 1994 to allow the highest achievers to stand apart.

## Significant recent changes to GCSEs

The most significant alterations, though, have occurred only in the past decade or so. Between 2005 and 2010, an increase in modular courses (with ongoing assessment) and changes to how non-exam content was marked, were among these. However, from 2010, controlled (i.e. supervised) assessment replaced coursework in several subjects, introducing tighter conditions, and reducing students' opportunities to obtain outside help (e.g. from parents).

In 2015, moves began to reform all GCSE subjects, English language, English literature and maths being the first. Most others changed to the new syllabus the year after, with exams scheduled for 2018. Any remaining ones changed to complete the conversion by the exams of 2019. The objective now is to grade solely by examination, with modular assessment resorted to only where unavoidable, as in performing arts subjects. Most higher and foundation tier papers disappear.

## The new grading system

The new grades run from 9 (at the top) to 1, allowing a finer differentiation than under the 8 strata offered by A*-G. The same proportion of students who in the past gained a C or above now receive a grade 4 or above; the proportion previously awarded an A or above get a grade 7 or above, while the top 20% of those receiving grade 7 or above get a 9.

## Fewer exam boards

With so many changes, the reduction of the once numerous examining boards and awarding organisations (to five) is welcome. These now are: the Assessment and Qualifications Alliance (AQA); Oxford and Cambridge and RSA Examinations (OCR); Pearson Edexcel; WJEC (formerly Welsh Joint Education Committee); and the Council for the Curriculum, Examinations and Assessment (CCEA).

In England, the examining boards operate under the jurisdiction of Ofqual (the Office of Qualifications and Examinations Regulation).

---

*'I feel better now I know that having to re-take maths needn't prevent me starting a level 2 diploma course.'* Year 11 student

---

## Some general concerns

Since their introduction, GCSEs have not lacked controversy. Some aspects of the debate have been of a general nature, but others over something specific. The first category includes the 'dumbing down' which some critics are convinced began from the moment GCSEs supplanted O levels. They believe that as well as reducing the theoretical content of many syllabuses, the change contributed to what is sometimes termed 'grade inflation'. This is apt to occur where norm-related marking (where a set percentage of examinees are awarded each of the available grades) is replaced by a criterion-based approach (with, in theory, no limit to how many gain high grades). Relatedly, government-set targets (aimed at creating league tables) influenced many individual schools to ensure significantly higher proportions of students ended up in the five A*-C grade category than would previously have merited this.

---

*'I was much less anxious about the most recent changes to GCSE after attending a talk at my son's school, and reading the handout for parents which they'd produced.'* Parent of Year 10 student

---

## Some particular concerns

Specific concerns have often been over individual subjects, or subject areas. One of these highlights the decline in students opting for foreign languages, not only at A level, but (where permitted) also at GCSE. With English so widely spoken, some students may see foreign language skills as being of little relevance to their plans, or think other subjects more likely to yield a high grade. However, if lack of enjoyment is the prompt, this raises questions over how such subjects are taught, and whether they might be made more attractive.

## How many subjects?

Students normally study at least five GCSE subjects. Three of these (English language, maths, and science) are compulsory, with a minimum of two more chosen from option groups. Although the national subject list has been trimmed considerably, it still features over 50. Many schools, especially those keen to maintain strong academic reputations, encourage their students to gain the English Baccalaureate. This is not an actual qualification, but represents a standard achieved by any student offering grades of 9-5 in English language, English literature and maths, and grades 9-4 in two sciences, a modern or ancient language, and either history or geography – seven subjects in all. Though this number reflects a commendable scholastic range, each year there are many students who exceed it.

---

*'I think our daughter's good GCSE results were due partly to a revision timetable which we helped her design, and encouraged her to stick to.'* Parent of Year 12 student

---

## Subject choice

Compulsory subjects apart, students can (within the confines of option groups) choose their remaining (probably from 3-6) subjects. Your son/daughter may find this agreeable in some respects, but less so in others. Certainly they're free to drop their poorest and/or least enjoyable subjects, but must commit to others for a further two years. Here are a few 'dos' and 'don'ts' which may help them accomplish this.

### Dos

Your son/daughter should ensure that they:

1. find out whether any career they have in mind requires GCSE subjects besides their compulsory ones
2. assess honestly whether the subjects they enjoy most are actually among their strongest
3. consider selecting wide-ranging GCSE subjects to keep open as many career avenues as possible
4. identify any discrepancies between assignment marks and exam grades in their current subjects, as nearly all GCSE assessment is now by exam.

### Don'ts

Your son/daughter should guard against:

1. opting for any GCSE subjects just because their close friends are
2. taking more subjects than necessary – seven or eight will normally keep open all post-16 option
3. overlooking any subject for GCSE which they may want (or need) to take at A level – in most cases, the first is required to begin the second.

## Information in school

Most schools introduce the topic of GCSE subject choice to students and their parents/guardians some way into year 9 (though some do this in year 8, as they begin the GCSE courses in year 9). Parents' evenings (or similar events) are held, where ample information is given, questions can be answered, and your son/daughter's current standard in each subject (and potential to continue with it) can be established and discussed with the appropriate teacher. This allows everyone time to think about each subject, and gives the student the opportunity to improve any requiring this. Choices are normally fixed by the end of year 9, however, to let students 'hit the ground running' at the start of year 10, the first of the two years devoted to GCSEs, also called Key Stage 4.

## Important rules

GCSEs will almost certainly be the first public exams your son/daughter has taken. To reflect their status, and in fairness to all candidates on exam days, rules relating to them are strictly observed. For instance, starting and finishing times are closely adhered to, so no student can afford to be late. The consequences for any candidate found cheating would be serious, and schools normally alert everyone well in advance as to what can be taken into an exam, or how a particular facility may be used. However, every student must still guard against carrying in by accident anything prohibited.

## Exam preparation

In the months leading up to GCSE exams, schools (and even individual teachers) may tackle preparation very differently. Some adhere to a revision timetable, with classes run to go over syllabus areas or topics in a set order, perhaps with exercises or homework designed to encourage an exam mentality, or accustom students to thinking and writing at a faster pace than usual. Other institutions (or staff) may be more relaxed, granting all year 11 students study leave several weeks ahead of the exam programme, with no obligation to be in school except to sit their own exams. Papers from previous years (normally available on exam board websites) can be consulted, to get a sense of the likely nature and standard of questions.

## Special requirements

During the exams themselves, allowances may be made for, or assistance offered to, students with learning difficulties, or restricted physically by a disability or injury. This help may take one or more forms, such as extra time (for instance, where a candidate is obliged to write slowly); an amanuensis (who writes down the answers which the student dictates), or a reader (normally for someone visually impaired). Where a reader or amanuensis is needed, the exam is usually taken in a separate room, in order not to disturb other candidates. It must be emphasised that any of the aids mentioned here must be approved in advance by the board concerned, and schools should ensure all necessary steps have been taken, to avoid problems for any candidate on exam days.

Requests for other kinds of help are likely to have the board's approval, provided they offer the candidate no unfair advantage. In the event of a student having to sit an exam while unwell, or an unforeseen circumstance arising which may adversely affect their performance, the school can ask the board to take this into account, one possible outcome being a percentage increase to the mark initially awarded.

## Times of exams and results

Students sit GCSE exams during April, May, and June each year, with results published in August, usually a week after those for A levels. Some examining boards (and even individual institutions) release results online, but most schools still ask candidates to collect them on their premises. This can be useful for students whose results prove insufficient for their intended progression, as it furnishes a rare opportunity to talk over their remaining options with teaching staff and (hopefully) an independent careers adviser.

## Subject and grade requirements for progression

Students normally require a minimum of five GCSEs at grades 9-4 (old A*-C) to progress to A levels or equivalent post-16 study or training, such as a level 3 diploma or an advanced apprenticeship. Any student obtaining a grade below 4 in English language or maths is usually strongly encouraged (and more often obliged) to retake it. However, provided they already have five at 9-4, most can do this alongside post-16 study or training, and are successful at the second attempt.

## Some specific requirements

To begin a particular subject at A level, you normally need at least GCSE grade 4 (sometimes 5) in that same subject. Typical exceptions to this are subjects widely available at A level, but offered at GCSE in only relatively few schools, instances being psychology, and certain foreign or ancient languages. In such cases, evidence of aptitude in a related subject may be required.

A student wanting to take science/maths A levels exclusively will almost certainly need GCSE maths, and at least two from physics, chemistry, and biology (and combined science/science). If your son/daughter's career ambitions are science, medical or engineering-related, they should (pre-GCSE choice) check the relevant degree course requirements of universities, as this may be the preferred (or even the only) route into their intended occupation.

*'I feel a lot more motivated to get good GCSE results since finding a college course I really want to do, and knowing the grades I'll need.'* Year 11 student

## What's the value of GCSEs?

GCSEs don't in themselves impart the skills sufficient to performing any job. Instead, their value lies in revealing each student's potential for further academic study, or for vocational preparation or training. Traditionally, the more academically able have stepped into A levels or (where offered) the International Baccalaureate (which consists of six subjects, in contrast to the two to four typical for A level). However, the high standards of level 3 diplomas and Advanced Apprenticeships are making the last two increasingly popular among those gaining good GCSE grades.

The nature and level of course or training for which college recruiters or employers consider an applicant suitable depends largely on their actual or predicted GCSE grades. Students therefore certainly shouldn't wait for their results before approaching organisations, and most begin applying to sixth forms, colleges, and training providers before or soon after Christmas. The majority receive conditional offers a few months before results day in August. The whole business of GCSE study and exams can prove as helpful to students as to recruiters, by encouraging them to pursue an existing plan, or inviting a change of direction. Students opting for academic study post-16 must recognise that this is at a deeper level, but can take comfort from the narrower subject-range, and knowing that a genuine interest in two or three subjects augurs well for success. Equally, a properly investigated job or career idea should allow those aspiring to a vocational path to step forward with confidence.

## Other things matter, too

Some schools place so much emphasis on the significance of GCSEs that students may be forgiven for overlooking the important role played by personal qualities and other kinds of knowledge in making progress. This rings especially true on the vocational side, where college or workplace recruiters look for evidence of candidates having researched areas of declared interest, and of having undertaken work experience.

## Length and number of exam

Most GCSE exams last from 90 minutes to two hours, and some are even under one hour. This is an improvement on their (often) longer predecessors, giving candidates a better chance of doing themselves justice by reducing the risk of tiredness. Whether a candidate sits more than one exam in a day largely depends on their subject options, as exam boards tend to spread out the compulsory ones. Their websites display timetables months in advance, so candidates know how many papers they'll sit, and are prepared for any necessary concentrations of effort.

---

*'I feel better now I know that having to retake maths needn't prevent me starting a Level 2 diploma course.'* Year 11 student

---

## Private candidates

The large majority of GCSE examinees attend a school or college, but there are exceptions. Most are students educated at home, privately tutored, or doing distance-learning courses (the last often being adults). Examining boards commonly refer to those in these categories as 'private candidates'.

Would-be private candidates should bear in mind some important things. Firstly, they must normally live in the UK, and take the exams at a UK centre. These are usually local schools and colleges whose own students are also taking their GCSEs there. There are hundreds of centres nationally, and each examining board's website features details of its approved ones. Few students need go far to attend one.

---

**Top tip from a careers adviser:** 'Year 11 is very demanding, study-wise, but it's vital that students research their options, too. It's usually best to attend open evenings and the like during the autumn term, before exam pressures mount, as they tend to from January on.'

**Top tip from a careers adviser**: 'For many vocational courses and apprenticeships, the right personal qualities and relevant work experience are at least as important as GCSE grades.'

## Useful websites

AQA:
www.aqa.org.uk/qualifications

CCEA:
www.ccea.org.uk/qualifications

OCR:
www.ocr.org.uk/qualifications

Ofqual:
www.gov.uk/government/organisations/ofqual

Pearson Edexcel:
http://qualifications.pearson.com/en/qualifications/edexcel-gcses.html

WJEC:
www.wjec.co.uk/qualifications

**Chapter 3**

# Years 10 and 11: career planning and choices

*Alison Dixon*

Career planning during years 10 and 11 is important. Your child must know about the different options available to them. That means **all** the options. The most important thing is that your son or daughter keeps their options open. It is very rare that a young person will know exactly what they want to do at that age. This chapter covers the choices your child will need to make and some of the common issues that occur.

## Help them with their choices

To make good choices, young people need to find out about themselves, what they are good at, what they enjoy (subjects at school and interests) and their current career ideas. You then need to help them to find out about the opportunities out there, the different routes they can take to achieve their objective and how and when to apply. Their school may have some careers interest guides (e.g. Cascaid, Morrisby, SACU or Higher Ideas), but there are also some free ones that can help, although the results of interest guides or careers questionnaires need to be talked through with an adviser. The Buzz Test is a very quick questionnaire to get them thinking, and others like 'allaboutcareers' and the careers quiz offered by Pearsons are good for getting ideas for careers (see websites listed at the end of this chapter). There are many others that you can find through Google, but take care as some are more useful than others.

## The importance of good advice

Your child's school or college may have other ideas of course. The form teacher or careers coordinator may think your child should go straight onto A levels in their sixth form and then to university, but nowadays this may not necessarily be the only 'gold-plated' route into a career. In fact, there are only certain careers where you need to have a degree and these include medicine, veterinary science, primary and secondary teaching, nursing, midwifery and physiotherapy.

You don't necessarily need a degree to work in law as there are different routes such as through entry as a paralegal and apprenticeships. The same goes for accountancy and some types of engineering as there are many trainee/apprenticeship schemes that can be entered at 18 (or even earlier), which can still lead to qualifications equivalent to a degree.

Although the traditional routes exist, they are changing as apprenticeships, and especially Degree Apprenticeships, are coming on stream.

Of course it's not just schools who may think that a full-time degree is the only way to progress in education. As a careers adviser, I often come across this with parents. There are many well-paid and fulfilling careers that don't require undertaking a full-time degree course as they can be entered via many other routes.

The same argument can be applied to qualifications. A levels may not be the best course of study for your child. You could consider BTECs, Cambridge Technicals, NVQs and the new T or Technical levels that are also coming on stream. Some courses are more vocational and geared to different careers.

## The labour market

This is another thing to look at. You need to know where the jobs are going to be. A few years ago there was a surplus of law graduates for example. Don't forget that your child may go into careers in the future that don't even exist now. Chapter 11 *The labour market: keeping up with the changes* and chapter 12 *The labour market: how to find the best information for you* will help you with this.

---

**Top tip:** Find out as much information as you can about all the options available and look at the labour market to see what jobs and careers are in demand.

---

Therefore it is important to consider other routes/alternatives and get good advice. If your child's school has a careers adviser, make use of them, as they have to be impartial. You can also get advice from the National Careers Service in England (or Careers Wales in Wales, My World of Work in Scotland and NI Direct in Northern Ireland). If you want to look at other courses available in the area, most are listed on the UCAS Progress website and if you want to look at apprenticeships there is a National Apprenticeship website (see also chapter 6 *Apprenticeships explained*). See the websites of these organisations listed at the end of this chapter.

---

**Top tip:** Get your son or daughter to discuss their options with as many people as possible… school, college, advisers, teachers etc… don't just take the school's advice as it may not be right for your child.

---

## The options

Below is a quick summary of the options that are available (you can read more about them in chapter 5 *Further education: why consider it?* and chapter 6 *Apprenticeships explained*).

- **Further education (FE)** – further full-time education could be in school, sixth form college or a college of further education. You can study for qualifications such as A levels, International Baccalaureate, BTECs, Cambridge Technicals, NVQs and qualifications offered by bodies such as City & Guilds.
- **Apprenticeships and work-based learning** – working towards an apprenticeship offers the opportunity to gain further work-based

qualifications as well as gaining work experience. Some apprenticeships (Higher or Degree Apprenticeships) lead to university-level study so can be an alternative to full-time higher education. A good example of this is the Advanced Apprenticeship in legal services which provides an alternative way to enter the legal world with the possibility for further professional training. There are also traineeships which teach the skills required to progress to apprenticeships and further training.
- **Voluntary work** is another option and it can be combined with learning and training.

---

**Top tip:** Encourage your son or daughter to keep their options open – you can usually apply to as many colleges, sixth forms and apprenticeships as you like – and you can apply to all of these and decide later on.

---

## Raising of the Participation age (RPA) or what happened to the school leaving date?

One thing that parents get confused about is the RPA (operating in England). Young people can legally leave school on the last Friday in June if they will be 16 by the end of the summer holidays. But the RPA is not actually raising the **school** leaving age, as young people can leave full-time education (either at school or college) at 16 but they must continue their education and training. They have the option to start an apprenticeship or traineeship, or spend 20 hours or more a week working or volunteering while in part-time education or training. The key thing is they are still learning and so the RPA helps young people with different learning styles. The RPA was formulated to ensure that any young person leaving full-time education has access to some training… they cannot therefore leave and go into a totally unskilled job. The local authority is responsible for promoting participation of young people, and tracking and supporting them.

Please note that in Scotland, Wales and Northern Ireland, the regulations are different:

- **Scotland:** If you turn 16 between 1 March and 30 September you can leave school after 31 May of that year. If you turn 16 between 1 October and the end of February you can leave at the start of the Christmas holidays in that school year.
- **Wales:** You can leave school on the last Friday in June, as long as you'll be 16 by the end of that school year's summer holidays.
- **Northern Ireland:** If you turn 16 during the school year (between 1 September and 1 July) you can leave school after 30 June. If you turn 16

between 2 July and 31 August, you can't leave school until 30 June the following year.

## Finance
### Get financial help with education costs
In England, some young people are eligible for support through a 16 to 19 Bursary Fund to help with education costs. Bursaries are for young people between 16 and 19 years and help with the costs of continuing with full-time education or training.

Schools, colleges and training providers are responsible for awarding bursaries to students. With the exception of the £1,200 bursaries for students most in need, they decide on the amount. They will also decide when bursaries are paid, and will set conditions that students should meet to receive a Bursary, for example, regular attendance.

In Scotland, Wales and Northern Ireland there is the Education Maintenance Allowance (EMA) to help with study costs.

---

*'My school told me it would be better for me to stay on for my A levels. I went to the college and they offered a much wider range of subjects and I liked the college straight away... the school were not very happy but I made my decision and am pleased with it.'* Emily, aged 17, studying at a sixth form college in East London

---

## Nothing is ever wasted... the myth of work experience
Work experience is not compulsory for any state school. As a careers adviser, I've talked to many young people who tell me their work experience was 'rubbish' or not the career area they wanted. It is a difficult task for any school or work experience provider to match a young person with their career area and indeed in some career areas there would be restrictions on young people working in that environment (e.g. a building site or factory).

However, when I talk to young people, I find that they have always learned something. and sometimes what they have learned is of great value. They may not be able to be a cashier at the bank they have gone to, but they will have seen how a business works, observed the dynamic of the office and perhaps experienced different management styles. They should have also learned the rules of 'how to behave' at work. These could be wide ranging and include timekeeping, dress code and even how to answer the phone. They may also realise the importance of networking and using your contacts. This could be applied to part-time and holiday jobs; you learn the skills of 'going to work' and in a paid job you will be learning how to manage your own money. (See also chapter 14 *Work experience: how to make the most of it.*)

## Banking your experience

I always tell young people that any work experience can be 'banked' and used later on in their career. They may be able to use contacts from their work experience to find a job or be able to give an example of how they managed to solve a particular problem and helped staff during their work experience. So even in year 11, your child could start building up a good CV. Never underestimate the importance of networking either as a chance contact could provide useful for a job later on. Don't forget that you can now join LinkedIn at the age of 13.

## Finally…

Finally, remember that this is just the start of your child's career journey. They are unlikely to stay in the same career all their lives and are likely to have many different careers and to retrain and upskill throughout their career. Their career plan will need to be reviewed as they gain experience and maturity along the way. So look at all options and keep your child's options open as much as you can.

# Useful websites

## Careers quizzes

Buzz Test:
https://icould.com/buzz-quiz/

All about careers:
www.allaboutcareers.com

Pearson:
www.pearson.com/uk/learners/secondary-students-and-parents/career-choices.html

## Other websites

National Careers Service:
https://nationalcareersservice.direct.gov.uk

Northern Ireland:
www.nidirect.gov.uk/campaigns/careers

Scotland:
www.myworldofwork.co.uk

Wales:
www.careerswales.com

UCAS Progress:
www.ucasprogress.com

Apprenticeships:
www.apprenticeships.gov.uk
www.gov.uk/apply-apprenticeship

School leaving age:
www.gov.uk/know-when-you-can-leave-school

16 to 19 Bursary Fund:
www.gov.uk/1619-bursary-fund

Education Maintenance Allowance (EMA) (Scotland, Wales and Northern Ireland):
www.gov.uk/1619-bursary-fund

**Chapter 4**

# Year 12: looking forward

*Mark Yates*

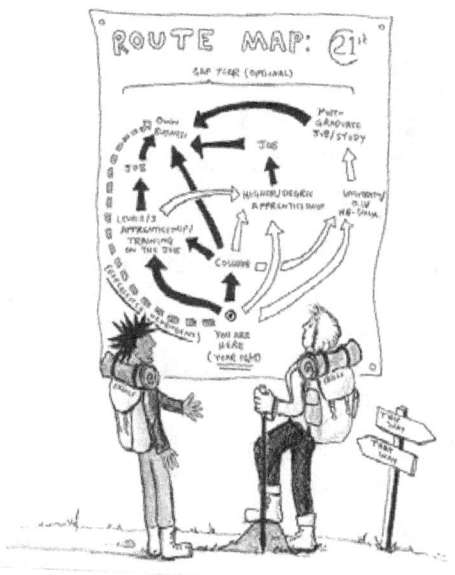

There are several options to consider for after year 12, which can lead in different directions. Moving on from year 11 is a big step academically, with the chance to specialise and take a step further towards building a successful career. This chapter will look at the options ahead, and reflect on how year 12 is a good springboard for considering future career pathways.

## So now that year 12 is under way

Year 11 will become a distant memory once year 12 has started, and the initial settling period has passed. But the change of focus, from doing numerous GCSEs to a smaller number of subjects or a single subject BTEC, or similar course, combined with the added maturity year 12 students develop, will hopefully start to focus minds about future possibilities.

It is important to realise that just because your son/daughter has got into year 12, this doesn't mean they can put their feet up and coast for a year before thinking about the A level exams in year 13. Schools will still be making predictions on UCAS forms in the first term of year 13 based on GCSE exam results and internal year 12 assessments. They will only be able to use evidence from year 12 and some of the autumn term to try to be as accurate as possible. If the courses being applied for are competitive, the effort and motivation shown during year 12 will definitely give teachers 'grounds for optimism' in predicting well.

Planning for after year 12/13 is important, and not to be ignored or put off for too long!

---

**Top tip:** Regularly review with your son/daughter how they are getting on, and how this could influence their future study and work choices.

---

## So what now? What are the options?

There are many options to consider for after year 12. Most students will carry on with year 13 to do the second year of A levels, IB, BTEC Extended Diploma, Pre-U etc, or whatever combination of these they are doing. Some students in year 12 may be doing a one-year level 2 course, in which case their options will be similar to year 11, such as an apprenticeship or a level 3 course – either at college or in the sixth form depending upon the grades they have achieved in their level 2, and in their maths and English GCSEs.

Some students will get towards the end of year 12, and realise that actually studying their current programme is not what they expected or want to carry on with. Some may come to this realisation with a 'nudge' from their tutor or head of year! All is not lost for these students though – in fact most, if not all, will gain something from having had this experience. These students will have several options too – one consideration will be to think through what has not gone well and why. This will help students to think about what would be better for them; many will go onto college to either restart a different combination of A levels, start a BTEC or get an apprenticeship. It is important to know that each year many students across the country will be restarting a level 3 course. This experience of their 'first' year 12 will often mature students considerably and make them a lot more focused and willing to work hard, often in an area they are a lot more interested in.

**Top tip:** It is important to help your son/daughter to think through why they are leaving, but at the same time realise that there is a successful 'future' out there for them. Being that year older at college won't be as big an issue as they might think it is.

## Planning for the future

Hopefully your son/daughter's positive experience of year 12 will be making them think about their future. There are definite things they need to start doing while in year 12 to plan for whichever option they want to do next. Here are some pointers.

## Going to university

- Start researching university options, e.g. by using the UCAS and Unistats websites.
- Visit open days, from April in year 12 to October in year 13. You will be surprised how many there are in September and October!
- Consider career ideas – they may need a specific degree.
- Plan any work experience/volunteering if needed, e.g. teaching, medical and social work related courses will require at least some volunteering. Some will want quite a bit!
- Some schools will want a draft personal statement done by the end of the summer term.

### Things to consider when researching university courses

There are lots of things that students can consider when researching their course options. Often the following factors will be ones most students will consider.

Firstly, with the course in mind, students will want to find out more about the content of the courses, the compulsory and optional units, any field trips involved (e.g. landscape design, horticulture and agriculture students will often go on site visits or study tours), any additional qualifications that can be gained as part of the degree, for instance sports students could get coaching or fitness training awards. It is worth finding out more about how many contact hours are involved, and the expectations around how many hours study will need to happen alongside this. Ask about who will be doing the teaching during their degree; will it include PhD students? Will the university bring in external specialists as hourly paid lecturers to share their expertise? Will students ever be taught by the well-known staff in the department or are they too busy with postgraduate students and their own research? Another factor is to look at the library facilities: how much are students able to access online, e.g. journals etc? What are the opening hours? Most universities won't want to encourage students to work through the night to meet deadlines, but will it be possible to access the library for extended periods before deadlines?

Your son or daughter will want to also give some thought to where the university study could lead them in the future. So it is worth asking about the range of jobs and organisations that past students have gone into from individual courses. And while past performance doesn't predict future outcomes, it can give a good idea of the sort of opportunities a course could lead to. For instance, how many will be successful in getting onto graduate schemes relating to the degree subject? What are the average salaries? Each university collected data from a survey called Destinations of Leavers from Higher Education (DLHE), now replaced by Graduate Outcomes. This information can be useful to look at, but don't just assume it will represent everything graduates can do! With this in mind, it is worth asking questions about how the university careers department will help your son/daughter during their time at university. Universities' careers departments are far better staffed and resourced than school or college careers departments (where you may get one person if you are lucky!) with teams of careers advisers, employer engagement staff, internship advisers etc.

---

**Top tip:** Some students will decide that they haven't got it 'right', and will change subjects in the first few weeks of year 12 or not carry on to year 13 – neither of these need to be seen as a 'disaster'.

---

There will be a plethora of information in different league tables. These are worth having a look at, but don't get too hung up on them; they all use data in slightly different ways to be different from each other. The data they use includes information about graduate destinations, salaries, postgraduate study (from the DLHE survey), National Student Survey (NSS) results (a student satisfaction survey of final-year undergraduates) and Teaching Excellence Framework (TEF – institutions are awarded Gold, Silver or Bronze, based on a mix of surveys already mentioned and staff research output). If all that has confused you with what seems like random letters being 'grouped together', you won't be the only one! So have a look at the league tables, try to understand how the rankings work and then research the options to decide which universities look best for your son/daughter. And don't forget that just because a course is say eight places up on another that it is necessarily a 'better' course/option, although it might well be!

Your son or daughter won't spend all their time studying while at university, or just planning their career! So it is definitely worth researching other factors too. What are the university buildings like; is it a campus or spread out around a city centre? Is your son or daughter interested in sport – what are the facilities and teams like? How active is the student union? They should provide ample opportunities to carry on with interests/hobbies/activities your son/daughter does now, while also providing the chance to try new things, by joining student societies; examples could include a parachuting society, chocolate appreciation society, re-enactment society… the list goes on, and is purely reliant on current students coming up with ideas and putting them into place!

Location is also an important factor. An increasing amount of students want to stay local so that they can live at home, for instance due to a part-time job. Others want to use the opportunity to live further away, perhaps to move to a larger urban area than where they currently live. Moving away can often mean having access to non-university activities, volunteering or acting opportunities being two examples.

There will be some students who have very specific reasons for applying to universities in a small geographical area. For instance, if a student is in a national sports squad, or in a professional/semi-professional team, and needs to access national training facilities or team coaching then this can limit choices. Or if a student has specific health or support needs that their current support network is best placed to carry on providing, this too can 'focus' applications geographically. And of course there will be other reasons why parts of the country are chosen, e.g. an interest in sailing or marine biology (being near the sea is helpful for both of these!), or hill walking – the list is endless!

## Apprenticeships and Degree Apprenticeships

Apprenticeships and Degree apprenticeships are increasingly popular. They are a great way to get specialist training and qualifications, up to masters level, in a wide range of occupational areas. This can range from catering, IT, surveying and engineering to newer opportunities for Degree Apprenticeships in nursing or management, amongst other areas. Degree Apprenticeships are what they 'say on the tin', i.e. a student will study for a degree while working as an apprentice and earning a salary.

If aiming at an apprenticeship, your son/daughter's career planning may need to be slightly more advanced than most students who are aiming for university. Is it insurance underwriting rather than accountancy, or retail management rather than hospitality management they are interested in?

When applications are made for apprenticeships, your son/daughter will be applying for a paid job, with a firm investing in their future, to help them do further specialist qualifications. Therefore they will want someone who knows exactly why they have chosen their particular occupational area – not just that it's a job in finance or engineering, or that it offers more disposable income than a student loan will!

Has your son/daughter got any work experience? This will help make their CV/application stand out – and could lead to job offers itself, if the experience is in the right area!

Make the most of any volunteering/part-time jobs, these can be very useful to demonstrate particular skills that an employer will want. For instance being a Brownie leader will show initiative and great problem solving, which will be highly sought after in several career areas, including hospitality/event management.

Start to find out about the local labour market. Where are the local opportunities? Which companies are out there? Is the transport to them easy? What can you find out about what they do? Many Local Enterprise Partnerships will have some labour market intelligence you could access.

## Finding a job

As a starting point, please read all the above comments relating to finding apprenticeships!

There are several questions that will need to be considered. Is entering the workplace a long-term prospect and the start of a student's 'professional' career? Or is it being done to gain experience in preparation for going to university in a year or two's time? For instance, working as a support worker before doing a mental health nursing degree, or gaining hospitality experience before doing an event management degree? Most employers like applicants to have 'commercial awareness', so time spent in the world of work can reap benefits later on.

Some students will have definitely had enough of study, and will 'just want' to get a job. Others might want to combine a desire to travel with a chance to earn some money while doing this (anyone for a season as a ski instructor or scuba diving instructor?). Others will want to work/volunteer to 'make a difference', e.g. doing youth and community work in an inner city, or undertaking marine conservation work or teaching English as a foreign language. The opportunities are limitless.

There are two important things to remember at this point. Firstly, having gained level 3 qualifications (i.e. equivalent to A levels), university will always still be an option later in life. In fact many students who go when they are older often think they get more out of the university 'experience' than those going at 18/19! Secondly, your son/daughter is likely to be working for roughly 50 years. During that time, they will change jobs numerous times, and most likely do something or work for an organisation that hasn't even been conceptualised yet! The most important issue will be that they start to develop their career management skills and 'mindset' to make the most of any opportunities that come their way. And just because they have not gone to university or started an apprenticeship straight after school, does not mean their career-related learning has stopped, or that they will not be offered opportunities for further study/work-based learning at a later stage. In fact, did you know that 'People aged 25 and over accounted for 46% of apprenticeship starts in 2016/17.' (House of Commons Briefing Paper Number 06113, 25 January 2018).

---

**Top tip:** Whatever students want to go onto in the future, it is important that they plan, prepare, and review.

---

## Gap year

For some students this will be about finding a job (see above) or to resit any exams while they apply/reapply to university.

The time between the end of exams (mid-June) to the start of university (often late September), can be a good chance to do something radically different; for instance, some considerable travelling, spending time doing a 'project', e.g. volunteering with wildlife or developing some unusual skills, perhaps in different parts of the world. Again this is sometimes done to 'support' a student's career thinking and preparation for university.

## In conclusion

Year 12 is an exciting and scary time for students. For many it is the first major decision they have taken about what they want to do, and is the first step towards a more independent life, not only in testing themselves further academically, but also starting to think about career and university options in more detail. And becoming old enough at some point during the year to start learning to drive. There will be a multitude of options to consider and information and advice coming from all angles. Along with their friends, they may think about spreading their wings to go all over the country, and even abroad – to study or, increasingly, to look for work/apprenticeships to move into instead of university. This is where your support, as a parent, being able to listen to your son/daughter, help them 'frame' the questions they need to ask, to challenge, nudge, and encourage all options to be fully explored will be much needed.

## Useful websites

UCAS:
www.ucas.com

Unistats course comparison website:
www.unistats.com

University and college open day directory:
www.opendays.com

Apprenticeships:
www.gov.uk/apprenticeships-guide

Milkround graduate recruitment website:
www.milkround.com

Prospects:
www.prospects.ac.uk

# Chapter 5

# Further education: why consider it?

## Mark Yates

This chapter is aimed at explaining about further education (FE) as an option for any young person. There are a range of courses and options available, which will be explored further. There are several myths about FE colleges to be 'busted' too!

## Why consider further education?

There are several reasons why young people and their parents consider this as an option. These include the following:
- the range of courses available is far more varied than sixth form, from entry (pre-GCSE) level to A level/BTEC Extended Diploma (and in some cases higher education courses too)
- an interest in training for a particular career, e.g. as a chef, hairdresser, mechanic, legal secretary, farrier
- an interest in a more general vocational course, e.g. health and social care, construction and the built environment, applied science or business studies
- wanting a fresh start in a new environment
- wanting to study in a slightly more adult environment
- being in a college with a few thousand other 16-19 year olds rather than 100-400 other sixth formers may appeal
- grades not being good enough for sixth form entry.

---

*'Choosing college has been a really good decision for me; I'm enjoying the course that I'm doing far more than sixth form.'* Simon, college student

---

## Facts and figures

Did you know…?

- There are 280 colleges, including: 14 land-based colleges; 10 specialist colleges; 68 sixth form colleges and 186 general FE colleges
- 11% of FE students are attending a higher education institute (i.e. a university) for their FE course
- Nationally there are 712,000 16 to 18-year-olds studying in colleges, in comparison to 424,000 in sixth forms. In addition to these figures, 77,500 are undertaking an apprenticeship through a college
- One third of under-19s who go onto university have studied in a college before going to university
- 72% of colleges were judged to be good or outstanding in their last Ofsted inspection.

(Association of Colleges Key Facts 2017/18)

These figures should hopefully demonstrate that FE is a successful route to take after year 11, 12 or 13!

Further education colleges can sometimes be seen as a great 'unknown', and thought of as aimed more towards students who haven't done well at school. While there is a grain of truth here, because of the range of courses available, the fact remains that colleges provide a huge range of qualifications and opportunities for students of all abilities and interests. In fact there are increasing numbers of students successfully applying to university from BTEC Extended Diplomas/Cambridge Technical qualifications, and most of these students will be applying from FE colleges. Not only do students have 'good' outcomes going onto university from FE, but students also go into a range of really good jobs too.

---

**Top tip:** Visit local colleges to compare the facilities, support and courses.

---

One of the great benefits of having a good local college to apply to is that, whatever results your son or daughter gets for their GCSEs, there will be a qualification level they can start with, which will give students the chance to progress well. Not only do students get to focus on an area they are particularly interested in, but there will also be plenty of opportunities to have contact with local employers. Having a number of good quality experiences with employers has been shown to increase students' chances of finding good quality work opportunities in the future! And many of the qualifications offered in further education colleges will have ample employer engagement as part of the course. Of course, some colleges, particularly sixth form colleges, will also offer A level pathways too, so it isn't just vocational or occupational courses on offer either.

Because of the variety of courses available, the range of learning methods will be more varied than in a traditional sixth form. So not only will there be some classroom-based learning, but learning experiences could, and will, also come from visiting employers, work experience or site visits (e.g. agriculture students visit a range of farms and farming technology shows). Training in a realistic work environment will often happen if it is appropriate – this could be a college kitchen, hair and beauty salon, crèche, stable yard or construction area.

---

**Top tip:** Ask what previous students have gone on to do after the course.

---

Having mentioned in general terms the variety of courses available, the following qualifications can be found in colleges across the country.

**Top tip:** Ask about any support requirements.

### A levels

These will be the same as in a sixth form! If a college or sixth form college offers A levels, there will often be a good a range of subjects available as you would find in a bigger sixth form. Students tend to take three A levels, sometimes four in some circumstances – usually for sciences and maths, with the student having lots of grade 9s and 8s (A* and A grades) at GCSE, to demonstrate they will cope with the extra demands of a fourth subject. Universities will make offers based on three A levels, so regardless of where you study them it is better to get three really good grades than four slightly worse ones.

**Top tip:** Don't assume further education is second best to sixth form as an option!

### Broad-based vocational courses

These qualifications are broadly vocational in their focus. Pearsons and City & Guilds offer BTECs/Advanced Diplomas and OCR offers Cambridge Technical qualifications. All these exam bodies offer qualifications at level 2 (GCSE standard) and level 3 (A level standard). The level 3 qualifications will have between 6 and 18 units each – depending on which award is taken, giving students a wide range of knowledge and skills to gain. 18 units is seen as equivalent to three A levels. BTEC also offer an entry level and level 1 (pre-GCSE), which will give students the chance to also work on their maths and English too, if needed.

These qualifications come in a variety of subject areas. Most commonly known about are courses such as business studies, art and design, engineering, health and social care and sport. But there are a range of more niche ones too, from agriculture, horticulture, animal/equine management, marine science and performing arts. At levels 1 and 2, students will usually concentrate on just one subject, the qualification will have enough units to fill their timetable – bar any extra maths and English they will need to do if they haven't got grade 4 at GCSE. For level 3, depending on the curriculum combinations being offered, students can either just do a full award, equivalent to three A levels or a mixture of BTEC/Cambridge Technical qualifications and A levels together.

---

**Top tip:** Check out the travel arrangements; some colleges will have buses they run from surrounding areas.

---

### Apprenticeships

The off-the-job training elements of doing an apprenticeship will occur either in an FE college or with a training provider. Both will provide the input and support needed to achieve the qualifications being worked towards. The apprenticeship opportunity itself will be something that needs applying for directly with the employer, and not through the college or training provider. Although sometimes colleges/training providers will know of local opportunities, as they will regularly be in contact with the employers they work with.

### Specific vocational training while at college full time

This is very similar to doing an apprenticeship, but without the employed status, and involves being at college 'full time'. Full time will often mean three or four days a week. All the skills and knowledge are learnt at the college, using their facilities so, for instance, trainee chefs, bricklayers or business admin students will use the specialist facilities to learn the skills needed.

Students will often have a preference for either an apprenticeship or full-time college for these types of opportunities; there will not always be a 'right' answer for which one is best. It will depend on the individual. For some, being in a work environment and doing an apprenticeship would be more appealing or more suitable, for others being in a college environment might meet their needs slightly more easily.

And the best advice if both appeal? Have a really good look at both ways of training, and perhaps apply for both a full time college course and an apprenticeship in case your son/daughter does not get an apprenticeship offer.

---

**Top tip:** Your son/daughter needs to be prepared to retake English and maths if they do not get a grade 4, whatever they apply for.

---

### Open days and how to apply

Colleges will have a variety of open days/evenings, where you can look around and talk to staff. These will be a great opportunity to find out more about possible courses, what is involved and what previous students have gone on to do. And if your son/daughter is receiving support at school for any reason, this support can usually be offered at college too. Especially if there is a Health and Social Care Plan in place!

While there are not often specific closing dates for college courses, unlike sixth forms, if the course is a popular one, it is worth applying earlier in year 11, for instance by Christmas. Popular courses tend to be ones like child care, plumbing, electrical installation, hairdressing and beauty therapy.

Once students have applied, they will be asked in for an interview. This is very much a two-way interview, in that the college staff will want to make sure the applicant knows what the course involves, and is motivated enough to put the work in, etc. But it is also a chance for students to find out about the course and the college, to see if they really measure up to expectations.

---

'Getting to specialise with horses and learn more about them has been great'.
Francesca, college student

---

## Myths
There is just enough space to quickly get rid of a few myths about further education.

- Colleges will have the same expectations as schools with regard to things like attendance, behaviour and achieving academically.
- While there is a more relaxed atmosphere, students are still expected to work hard, get homework done and 'live up to' high standards.
- Colleges face the same OFSTED inspection regime and financial constraints as schools, so will take a similar approach to bad behaviour and wanting to make sure students are on the right course.
- Colleges will have good student support available, to help students with a variety of support needs. They will often also have a careers adviser or two on the staff.
- Just because college courses often require attendance for just three or four days a week, it does not mean that they are 'easier' or that assignments and study don't need to happen while not at college.
- Choosing a broad vocational area does not mean your son/daughter will be 'stuck' with that as the only future work area they can get into. I have known an equine student successfully go onto a psychology degree as one example of a change of direction. There will be numerous other examples of 'changes of direction' that college staff will be able to give you.

## Useful websites

UCAS:
www.ucas.com

Information about further education courses:
www.gov.uk/further-education-courses

Apprenticeships:
www.gov.uk/apply-apprenticeship

Pearson further education and vocational resources:
www.pearsonschoolsandfecolleges.co.uk/learner-and-parent-fe-and-vocational/learner-and-parent-fe-and-vocational.aspx

City & Guilds:
www.cityandguilds.com

OCR Cambridge Technical qualifications:
www.ocr.org.uk/qualifications/by-type/cambridge-technicals

**Chapter 6**

# Apprenticeships explained

*Cerys Evans*

Apprenticeship opportunities have been making the headlines in recent years, but they can be tricky to find and, in some cases, can be more competitive than the more well-known academic options. As a result, parents of young people considering a work-related option might have questions about whether an apprenticeship is the right choice for their son or daughter. Here, we set out to answer the questions and address any concerns.

## What is an Apprenticeship?

Apprenticeships have existed since the Middle Ages. The notion of a master craftsman training up a young successor is well-known. Today, things have moved on considerably with the range of roles expanding far beyond traditional trades to incorporate almost any skilled job.

An apprenticeship provides the opportunity to learn at work, rather than solely through education. Its benefits are many, including the chance to build experience, as well as skills and knowledge. Apprentices get supported entry to the workplace with mentors they can turn to when help or advice is required.

Apprentices earn a wage for the work that they do, get any qualifications paid for (even when that qualification is a university degree that typically costs thousands of pounds per year). In addition, they complete their programme having gained substantial work experience and ready to take their next step on the career ladder.

There is no expectation that an apprentice already knows how to do the job they are training for, but applicants for apprenticeships do need to be ready for the workplace and keen to learn. Particularly on some of the higher-level opportunities, there is an expectation that they will be adding value to the company from early on.

An apprenticeship should last at least one year, with some of the highest-level schemes taking five or six years to complete.

Apprentices learn through work to develop the knowledge, skills and behaviours related to their job role. In some cases they will also work towards a formal qualification. Typically, an apprentice spends 80% of their working week in the workplace, with 20% spent completing off-the-job training.

Off-the-job training might take the form of day-release, with the apprentice attending a local college, university or training centre for one day per week. In some cases, apprentices will learn through block-release, studying for a week or more at a time, maybe at a specialist training centre or university. If a stay away from home is required, the employer will provide support with this. Online learning might be another element of an apprentice's learning, with some employers opting for a combination of methods, known as blended learning.

As any studies undertaken relate to the work being done, apprentices (and their employers and trainers) often report on the positive progress they make with their learning.

Apprentices have a contract of employment and the rights of an employee, including holiday pay. apprentices aged under 19 (or those aged 19 or over in the first year of an apprenticeship) will receive a minimum wage of £3.90 per hour (April 2019). Apprentices aged 19 or over who have completed the first year of their apprenticeship should be paid the relevant minimum wage. See www.gov.uk/national-minimum-wage-rates for the latest figures.

In practice, many employers pay more than the minimum and in some industries, such as engineering or finance, a substantially higher wage is possible. For apprentices working towards the higher-level qualifications, starting wages in excess of £12,000 per annum are commonplace with some companies paying out closer to £20,000.

## What's on offer?

The range of job roles that can be accessed through an apprenticeship has grown dramatically in recent years. The Government has been working with employers to develop and extend the range of roles on offer. There is no apprenticeship for doctors, but perhaps this is only a matter of time; most other job roles are offered or in development. Opportunities to become a qualified nurse, teacher and police officer are all under development, with some schemes already underway. It is possible to become an aeronautical engineer, solicitor or quantity surveyor by taking an apprenticeship, as well as roles like teaching assistant, roofer or veterinary nurse.

## Location

Although the range of apprenticeships is far broader than it was, your son or daughter will need to find out whether the types of roles that interest them are available locally. Fashion-related apprenticeships are rare in Sheffield, but more likely in London, for example. Apprenticeship opportunities tend to reflect the needs of the local or regional labour market. You can find out more in chapter 11 *The labour market: keeping up with the changes*. Locally, you could seek advice from the careers staff at your son or daughter's school, college or local careers service.

Some young people move away from home to pursue apprenticeships, but this isn't widespread. Larger firms with higher-level opportunities may offer the wages and the practical and social support for relocation, but most companies aren't able to do this.

## Types of Apprenticeship

To find out more about the types of apprenticeship available, go to the national apprenticeship pages for your son or daughter's home nation:

- England:
  www.gov.uk/education/types-of-apprenticeships
- Scotland:
  www.myworldofwork.co.uk/getting-job/apprenticeships
- Wales:

www.careerswales.com/en/jobs-and-training/job-seeking/vacancy-search/what-is-an-apprenticeship/
- Northern Ireland: www.nidirect.gov.uk/articles/types-apprenticeships.

## Apprenticeship levels explained

Across the UK, apprenticeships are available at a range of levels with all nations offering opportunities for young people aged 16 and over, as well as options for young people aiming for university-level qualifications.

Depending on where you live, there can be some differences in the details and the terminology used to describe apprenticeships. Much of this will not make a huge difference to your son or daughter, but it helps to be aware of it.

In Scotland, in an attempt to narrow the gap between the classroom and the world of work, students are offered the opportunity to work towards a Foundation Apprenticeship starting in S5 at school. It takes two years to complete, is the same level as a Higher and counts as one subject choice. Students can specialise in one of a range of subjects, including hardware and system support; social services and healthcare; or food and drink technologies.

**Intermediate Apprenticeships** offer qualifications at level 2. In Scotland, they're known as Level 2 Modern Apprenticeships, or Level 2 Apprenticeships in Wales. In Northern Ireland, your son or daughter might start with a traineeship instead; this includes a workplace component but they will not necessarily be classed as an employee.

---

**Top tip:** Traineeships are available in England and Wales for students wanting to move into the workplace but needing a bit more support or experience to do so. Find a traineeship at www.gov.uk/find-traineeship or www.careerswales.com/en/cap/traineeships

---

Entry requirements vary for apprenticeships at this level, but typically GCSEs grades 3/D or National 4 qualifications will be required as a minimum. Even where no qualifications or grades are specified, applying with some qualifications can make it easier for your son or daughter to make it through to the interview stage.

In some practical roles, such as bricklaying or hairdressing, apprentices are expected to start at intermediate level to develop the basic skills before they can progress higher.

**Advanced Apprenticeships** (or Level 3 Apprenticeships/Modern Apprenticeships) offer qualifications comparable to A levels, or Scottish Highers and Advanced Highers.

GCSE grades 4/C or above and National 5 qualifications, particularly in English and maths, would tend to meet the typical entry requirements. Some roles will expect certain grades in other subjects too.

Not quite ready for an apprenticeship? In England and Wales, your son or daughter could consider a traineeship to build experience of the workplace and prepare for employment.

**University-level Apprenticeships**

If your son or daughter wants to gain university-level qualifications through an apprenticeship, they should look out for:

- Higher and Degree Apprenticeships in England
- Graduate Apprenticeships in Scotland
- Higher Apprenticeships in Wales
- Higher Apprenticeships in Northern Ireland.

In all four nations, apprentices can work towards a range of qualifications, from Higher National Diplomas (HND) and foundation degrees to undergraduate and postgraduate degrees. They will work towards the same qualifications as students studying full-time at universities or higher education institutions, and will graduate in the same way.

Typically, employers will be looking for grades C and above from A levels or Highers, similar to the grades required to apply to most universities. In addition, they're looking for applicants with the drive, focus and commitment to contribute to the workplace and balance work and study; essentially, employers want the full package.

**Age limits for apprentices**

Apprentices should be at least 16 and have left school before they start an apprenticeship (with the exception of school-aged students working towards Foundation Apprenticeships in Scotland alongside their schooling).

There is no upper age limit for apprenticeships in the UK, although the funding that an employer receives might differ depending on the age of the apprentice, whether they have left care or have an education, health and care (EHC) plan. In Northern Ireland, you can still start an apprenticeship at 25 or over, but the job sectors are more limited.

**Top tip:** Graduates can now opt for an apprenticeship too, as long as they are developing new skills and the apprenticeship is significantly different from their previous qualifications.

## Opportunities for applicants with disabilities

Look out for Disability Confident employers (displaying a Disability Confident logo on their vacancies or application forms). If your son or daughter identifies as disabled when applying for these vacancies they should be offered an interview, provided they meet minimum entry requirements. Of course, regardless of the logo, all employers must make reasonable adjustments to ensure that workers (including apprentices) with disabilities, or physical and mental health conditions, aren't disadvantaged when doing their jobs.

Disability Rights UK provides a useful *Into Apprenticeships* guide for disabled people and their parents. See: www.disabilityrightsuk.org/intoapprenticeships

**Top tip:** If your son or daughter isn't ready for an apprenticeship, look out for a supported internship to help them prepare. A supported internship is aimed at young people with an education, health and care (EHC) plan who want to move into employment and need extra support to do so.

## Apprenticeship myths

There are plenty of myths out there around what an apprenticeship is all about and where it can and can't lead. Here, we set out to dispel some of them.

### Cheap labour

Apprenticeship wages tend to be lower than the full salary for the relevant job role, so does this mean that apprentices are nothing more than cheap labour for employers?

It is worth considering that apprentices require support throughout their training before they become competent in their chosen role; this incurs costs for the employer. In addition, unlike most employees, apprentices spend 20% of their working week completing off-the-job training, and may gain a recognised qualification. Add to this that plenty of employers pay above the minimum wage, and the idea of an apprentice being a cheap option starts to diminish.

**No future after an Apprenticeship**
Some parents worry that at the end of an apprenticeship, their son or daughter will be left with nothing. On the contrary, most employers train up apprentices with the intention of keeping them on with the company and the vast majority remain with the same employer upon completion. For longer apprenticeships in particular, there is little business sense in training someone up for four or more years, if you then intend to start anew with another apprentice.

Once an apprenticeship is completed, over 90% of apprentices remain in work or further training, according to a February 2017 briefing from the Education and Skills Funding Agency.

---

*'I would consider an apprenticeship for my children if it gave them the right experience for the career they wanted, and it was accredited properly. I also think it would make a difference if it was with an employer that I recognise and trust too.'* Gill Wood, parent

---

After they complete their training, apprentices might also choose to look for other opportunities where the qualification, experience and skills they have developed will be in demand; this might be within the same role or industry, or something completely different.

Be warned: some employers will expect an apprentice to stay with them for a certain length of time once the programme is completed; perhaps three or more years for some higher-level opportunities. This should be clearly explained in the apprentice's contract.

In companies and industries with a strong history of apprenticeships, the idea of starting as an apprentice and moving into senior leadership is fairly common. Companies such as Rolls Royce are testament to this. A recent influx of chartered management Degree Apprenticeships means that this trend looks set to continue.

---

**Top tip:** Apprentices on Degree or Graduate Apprenticeships will miss out on many of the experiences of traditional university life, but should find themselves graduating debt-free and ready for the workplace.

---

**Full-time university is the better option**
There is a commonly-held belief that graduates earn more than apprentices, but this isn't always the case. In fact, the very best apprenticeships (at level 5 or

higher) result in greater lifetime earnings than degrees from many universities. See *Levels of Success* from the Sutton Trust to find out more: www.suttontrust.com/research-paper/levels-of-success-apprenticeships-earnings/

Some would argue that a Degree Apprenticeship is now the route of choice for those who know the career direction they wish to take. The option of several years of experience, no university debts and a stronger foothold in the graduate labour market is looking increasingly attractive, particularly now that some of the more elite universities, including the University of Cambridge, are recognising the value of offering Degree Apprenticeships.

Having said that, the university route tends to work best for young people who haven't decided on a career path or don't feel ready for the workplace and want the independence and breadth of higher learning that university offers.

Parity between the work-based and academic routes is some way off yet, but the gap does appear to be narrowing, and the introduction of Degree or Graduate Apprenticeships seems to have contributed to this.

It is worth noting that the two pathways are far from equal in numbers. According to UCAS, around 440,000 UK students started full-time degrees at the UK's universities in 2017, but only a fraction of that number started on higher-level apprenticeships; 36,000 in England in 2016/17 according to Government data, although higher-level apprenticeships are growing.

## Finding an Apprenticeship

If the prospect of an apprenticeship looks appealing, here's how your son or daughter can find one.

### What's needed to get an Apprenticeship?

Maturity, work-readiness and the right attitude will get your son or daughter a long way towards getting an apprenticeship, but that isn't the full story. A combination of academic qualifications, practical experience, the ability to talk about strengths and skills, and the drive to get started in the workplace tend to provide a winning combination. In reality, many applicants need help addressing some of these selling points and it certainly pays to prepare.

As with any job, there is an element of competition in securing an apprenticeship. Some vacancies are more fiercely contested than others, with the most prestigious opportunities receiving hundreds of applications per place.

Opportunities in sport or animal care, for example, can be in short supply, so when vacancies appear, applicants will need to show their commitment to the job area, often through relevant experience.

When applying for an apprenticeship, as with any job, a certain level of professional etiquette is required. If your son or daughter is 15 or 16 and just leaving school, this might be new to them, so it is worth talking to them about what most employers will expect.

**Apprenticeship-ready checklist**
Check that your son or daughter can offer the following:

- a CV
- a professional-looking email address
- the ability to pick up the phone and have a conversation with someone they don't know
- the skills to respond to a professional email
- willingness to research the company and role before applying
- the ability to accept constructive criticism and deal with some rejection.

---

*'I walked into the interview and discovered that I was the youngest person there. The others seemed far more experienced than me and I found it a bit off-putting initially.'* 16-year-old applicant, design engineering Advanced Apprenticeship

---

Applicants to Higher and Degree Apprenticeships are often expected to go through recruitment processes typically undertaken by graduates, including video interviews, online assessments, psychometric tests and assessment centres.

---

*'I have lots of work experience, I'm studying relevant subjects and I had made the effort to prepare and research the company. The video interview was still daunting. I was given a scenario to respond to and a time limit in which to record my response. I felt self-conscious talking to myself and some of the scenarios were very challenging.'* 18-year-old applicant, Chartered Manager Degree Apprenticeship

## Five key characteristics of successful apprentices
Successful applicants to apprenticeships tend to have certain attributes in common:

1. enthusiastic
2. determined
3. prepared
4. mature
5. focused.

## Searching for an Apprenticeship
Unlike standard college and university applications, the process of applying for an apprenticeship can be far more complicated.

---

**Top tip:** Applying for an apprenticeship requires time, focus and organisation.

---

## When to look
For higher-level opportunities, companies might start recruitment processes up to a year in advance, mirroring university applications.

Unlike UCAS applications, apprenticeship vacancies can appear at any time and application isn't standardised, so young people might have to get used to a range of application formats.

Applicants should start looking in the autumn before they plan to start work and continue checking websites weekly or fortnightly thereafter.

---

**Top tip:** Encourage your son or daughter to look out for company insight days or experience days to find out more about the organisation and strengthen future applications.

---

Companies recruiting for advanced or intermediate-level schemes might take applications a little later in the year. Some large firms who recruit apprentices annually tend to open for applications before Christmas, but most start recruiting from January onwards. Many small or medium-sized businesses might not start the process until after Easter. Again, registration on key websites and regular trawls of vacancies helps to ensure that opportunities don't get missed.

If applying from school, sixth form or college, it is quite common for young people to have a bit of a wobble around March or April. Typically, at this time of year, their friends might be receiving offers from sixth forms, colleges or universities, while they might still be looking for the right opportunity. For this reason, and as a result of the highly-competitive nature of some vacancies, it always helps to have a solid back up plan.

**Where to look**

There are a range of apprenticeship recruitment websites to choose from, but most opportunities should be advertised on the national apprenticeship websites listed below.

England:
www.apprenticeships.gov.uk and
www.findApprenticeship.service.gov.uk

Scotland:
www.apprenticeships.scot

Wales:
https://ams.careerswales.com

Northern Ireland:
www.nidirect.gov.uk/services/search-Apprenticeship-opportunities

For a handy list of Higher and Degree Apprenticeship vacancies in England, see:
www.gov.uk/government/publications/higher-and-degree-apprenticeship-vacancies

Alternative websites include:

UCAS Career Finder:
https://careerfinder.ucas.com

All About School Leavers:
www.allaboutschoolleavers.co.uk

Rate My Apprenticeship:
www.ratemyApprenticeship.co.uk

Get My First Job:
www.getmyfirstjob.co.uk

It is also worth searching on the websites of companies that are of interest to your son or daughter. Look for the **careers, early careers, apprenticeships** or **working for us** pages.

For smaller businesses, look out for local companies operating in your area and consider making a speculative approach. You could enlist the help of local colleges or training providers who may be able to advise on potential employers.

Don't underestimate the value of your network of contacts; you could start with friends and family to see if they know of any upcoming opportunities.

If your son or daughter decides that an apprenticeship is right for them, you can get support and information on local or regional opportunities from the careers staff at your son or daughter's school, college or local careers service.

## Chapter 7

# UCAS personal statements: what are universities really looking for?

### Alan Bullock

While there is increasing diversity in the routes and pathways young people now follow at 18, more than 600,000 people apply for higher education each year through UCAS. As part of the process they are required to write a personal statement, which sometimes gives cause for anxiety. The aim of this chapter is to shed light for you as a parent on what university admissions tutors really look for in the statement and, hopefully, to help you to help your son or daughter approach the process with positive enthusiasm, not fear and trepidation.

## Summary of the UCAS Apply process

Students apply online using the UCAS Apply system and most applicants do so through their school or college. A UCAS application consists principally of:
- personal details
- up to five choices of course
- school(s) or college(s) attended since the age of 11
- qualifications taken and to be taken
- personal statement.

The school or college then adds an academic reference and estimated grades and submits the application to UCAS.

For applicants who have left full-time education in the past couple of years or so, it is normally in their best interests to apply through their previous school or college, if possible, rather than to apply independently.

The closing date for those students who are applying to Oxford or Cambridge, or for medicine, dentistry or veterinary medicine, is 15th October and for most other courses it's 15th January. However, many courses still have vacancies after 15th January, and therefore it is possible to apply later, although a student's school or college may discourage that.

After the application has been received, some courses at some universities will respond quickly with an offer, an invitation to attend an interview or open day or, occasionally, a rejection. Others may wait until after the 15th January deadline, using the 'gathered field' approach. Once all replies have been received, UCAS will confirm the date by which applicants need to decide which offers, if any, to hold as their Firm and, optionally, Insurance choice. Thereafter the Extra and Clearing processes enable unplaced applicants to make further applications, one at a time, if they want to. Also, if applicants change their mind about the choices they've made, it's possible to decline their offers and re-apply to one more course through Extra or Online self-release into Clearing. In addition, a process called Adjustment allows a small number of applicants to 'trade up' in August if their results are better than anticipated.

## Making UCAS choices

In UCAS you can apply for a maximum of five courses. Most applicants apply for the same or similar courses at five different institutions, although it is by no means compulsory to do so and there are many circumstances in which an applicant might be justified in taking a less conventional approach. Read on to find out more!

Many applicants also find it appropriate to balance their choices so that they include at least one aspirational choice and one fallback choice amongst the five, although this too is something that depends very much on the individual and their specific circumstances. Some applicants may also decide not to use all five choices, for example if they don't want to move away from home and only have one or two realistic choices open to them. It is also possible to add choices later in the process if they choose not to use all five at the outset.

At the time of writing (2018), the demographic curve in the UK is such that there is a dip in the population of 18 to 20-year-olds. This means that a significant proportion of courses and universities are in 'recruitment' rather than 'selection' mode. Because of this it may be quite sensible for applicants to be positive and ambitious in their choices. Having said that, some popular courses and universities remain as competitive as ever. Therefore, three key messages for students are:

- don't assume anything
- do your research
- and don't leave it too late to start your research

## Taking pride in the UCAS application

The best applicants approach and complete their application carefully and thoroughly. For example, if in doubt about how to complete any of the questions or sections, click on Help. By answering everything in good English, paying attention to spelling, punctuation, correct use of capitals and so on, an applicant will come across as someone who is keen to impress and who takes pride in doing things correctly.

## The personal statement – don't stress!

The personal statement, however, is the section for which there are few rules and therefore great scope for applicants to differentiate themselves from other applicants and make a strong case for being offered a place on their chosen courses. For many students every year it's a source of anxiety and stress, but it need not be!

Rather than leave it until last, it makes good sense to start thinking about the personal statement early in the process. Many students take several weeks or months to gradually draft and enhance it, although I have known some to write it in one go.

Let's now look at what's needed and how students can shine.

## Personal statement basics

The main rules are:

- 47 lines maximum
- 4,000 characters maximum (**including spaces**)
- 1,000 characters minimum
- you can't underline, indent or use bold or italics.

Structure is important and using paragraphs is advisable. However, if you leave a line between paragraphs, it counts as one of your 47. It's a matter of personal choice whether to leave a line or not.

## How important is the personal statement?

It's especially important for:

- high-demand courses and high-demand universities
- 'professional' courses, where in effect you're applying for the profession as well as the course.

For some 'professional' courses the statement might even be scored against a university's selection criteria. So, for a degree like physiotherapy, for example, it's especially important to know what attributes or experiences are needed and to reflect on these in the statement.

Alternatively, the personal statement might emerge as a crucial or deciding factor at 'Confirmation' in August if the applicant doesn't quite meet the conditions of the offer they received from their Firm or Insurance choice universities. In this situation, a university may still confirm the place, especially if their personal statement has impressed them.

On the other hand, if the applicant's estimated grades are sufficient and any other entry requirements are met, some courses at some universities might only give the statement a cursory glance. Also, some admissions staff urge applicants not to get stressed about the statement. Advice I have heard from some courses includes:

> '*We rarely reject a student because of a personal statement*'
> '*Don't see it as a scary obstacle where you have to sell yourself nor worry that it must conform in some way; just see it as an opportunity to show your enthusiasm for the subject*'.

## Useful advice for your son or daughter

Below are some useful pointers, including some from university admissions staff themselves.

### Don'ts...

DON'T exaggerate, waffle or repeat yourself.
DON'T plagiarise – it will be detected by UCAS software.
DON'T make spelling, grammar or punctuation errors:
 *'One mistake can lead to rejection.'* (law)
DON'T use quotations for effect:
 *'We ignore quotes, so those lines are wasted.'*
 *'OMG, not David Attenborough again.'* (geography)
 *'We see lots of Ghandi quotes (groan, sigh)'*
 *'I'm fed up with Muhammad Ali quotes.'* (sports science)
 *'I would rather you quote your grandad than Confucius.'*
 *'I don't care what Locke thinks, I want to know what you think.'* (law, again)
DON'T be smarmy, or patronising: 'It will be an honour to be accepted at your esteemed university' won't impress.
DON'T use pretentious, stilted or archaic vocabulary, even more so if it's spelt incorrectly. I once read: 'It was in Year 10 that my love for maths came fourth'.

### Dos...

DO focus on why you want to study the course(s).
DO **reflect** on the skills, interests, experiences, ideas, qualities, attributes or aspirations you will bring to the course, both academic and personal.
DO convey your enthusiasm for learning and a passion for the course... but preferably without using the word 'passion'.
DO use formal rather than colloquial language, but also write naturally, as if you're speaking to the admissions tutor face to face.
DO search course websites for tips and advice. For instance, Bristol's website has an 'admissions statement' for every degree discipline, including guidance on what is sought in the personal statement. And as one medical school said: *'We tell you what we want on our webpage, but most applicants don't look'*.

### 30 more tips from universities

- Be yourself and make sure your enthusiasm for the course shines through.
- We want to hear your voice.
- If an adult has helped you write it, we can tell.
- There's no such thing as a model statement.

- Most of all, we want people who are **enthusiastic** about the course.
- Tell us what you think, not just what you do.
- We're looking for a reason to accept you, not reject you.
- Be formal, but in your own words.
- Be original, but not too original – the English applicant who wrote in rhyming couplets didn't impress.
- The best statements are those that are truly genuine…
- The worst are those that don't focus enough on why you want to study the course and that fail to show an understanding of it.
- Show that you understand something about the course you're applying for – for example, we quite like it if you give your opinion on something.
- If you're dyslexic, don't hide it. How have you overcome it?
- Write in paragraphs. I want to be engaged by it. Every section should make me wonder what's coming next.
- For academic courses, the best statements address the **super-curricular** (your outside reading or other independent learning beyond the syllabus).
- Do include the extra-curricular too, especially if it's unusual, but make it relevant to the subject in some way or use it to evidence relevant skills or attributes.
- If you've overcome challenges or difficulties, show us.
- Our pet hate is when applicants tell us why they chose each of their A level subjects.
- The personal statement is your one chance to speak to the admissions tutor.
- Avoid clichés (especially *'from a young age'* or *'since I was a child'*).
- Be selective about what you write – less is more.
- If you've had relevant experience, we want you to **reflect** on what you learned from it.
- What skills does the course require and how can you **evidence** them?
- It's your commitment to the subject we want to know most about, more than Duke of Edinburgh, flute or being netball captain. Show that you've engaged with the subject… for example by reflecting on your EPQ or a public lecture you attended or why you follow a particular academic on Twitter…
- We hate poor spelling, punctuation and grammar, not using capital letters for names and overuse of quotations or clichés. What we do want to see is genuine engagement with the subject. And we don't want gimmicks – the person who wrote their statement in a heart shape was rejected.
- There's no perfect statement, but structure is important. And we don't necessarily need to know about your career plans unless they're an important part of your motivation for doing the course.

- Avoid using sophisticated language that you don't fully understand.
- If you're applying for a joint or combined course, we want to know about both subjects.
- If you're applying for deferred entry, tell us about your gap year plans in one sentence.
- Be aware that what you say in your statement may come up in an interview.

## Advice from universities on how to stand out from the crowd

Tell us something that makes you stand out.
We're busy; grab our attention, what makes you different?
We like you to be different, but not **too** different.
Weird is not a selling point.
Off-the-wall won't work.
Don't be outrageous – you'll stand out, but not in a good way.

## So, a better way to stand out is to...

Convey genuine enthusiasm and motivation ...
...starting with a strong opening sentence that engages because it's interesting and personal, not gimmicky.
Remember, this isn't 'The Apprentice'.

## Oxford and Cambridge: three tips from admissions tutors

1. *'Super-curricular exploration is vital for a competitive application and the best personal statements are a reflective narrative of your academic motivation and experiences beyond the curriculum. What have you watched/read/engaged with? What was new to you about it? What were you compelled to do next? What did you learn from this? What was difficult or challenging about it or what made you look at the subject from a new perspective?'*

2. *'We would love to know what you want to question about your chosen subject or what concerns you about it.'*

3. *'The worst personal statements are polished but boring.'*

## It's easier if the five choices are all for the same course...

Quite simply this is because applicants can only write one statement to cover all five choices in their UCAS application and, for it to be effective, each person who reads it will normally expect all of it to be relevant to them in some way. However, what if your son or daughter's five choices aren't all the same? Possible solutions are:

- If there are slight differences, or they've chosen joint or combined degrees with slightly different subject combinations, this shouldn't be a problem. Just try to make everything as relevant as possible to all five choices.
- If there are big differences, they should seek advice from teachers, advisers or – better still – from the universities themselves. They could blend it, so that all of it is relevant to all five choices, or be honest in it and explain why they've chosen different courses. However the latter approach especially could be risky if applying for competitive courses.
- If one of the choices is completely different, do ask the university concerned. They might consider a separate statement sent directly to them or they might advise you just to include a subtle hint.
- Or if applying for medicine, dentistry or veterinary medicine, for which you're restricted to a maximum of four choices, then some other courses may be happy to be the fifth choice even though your statement needs to focus on your main choice course. In this case, it's a good idea to ask the fifth choice before you include it.

## Balancing academic and extra-curricular content

Courses in 'academic' subjects, such as history, physics, philosophy, maths, English, geography or languages, generally prefer to see more emphasis on academic and super-curricular interests (75%ish).

'Professional' courses on the other hand, such as nursing, dentistry or primary teaching, where you are very much applying for the career not just the course, will want much more reflection on your 'experience' or relevant voluntary work or observation.

However, courses in other 'vocational' subjects such as law, engineering, politics or architecture, may not need as much 'experience' as you expect – it depends on what is motivating you to study the subject.

## Be specific

Avoid making bland, unsubstantiated claims like:
    *'I have always wanted to study history.'*
    *'I was born to dance.'*
    *'I genuinely believe I am a highly-motivated person.'*
    *'Being a prefect has shown my leadership skills.'*

Instead, give **specific** examples that provide **evidence**, like:
    *'Reading X's autobiography taught me that...'*
    *'A podcast on climate change led me to question accepted truths about...'*
    *'My prefect duties have given me the confidence to...'*

*'Through taekwondo I have learned the value of...'*

## Openings and endings

*'Using hackneyed phrases is not the best way to stand out.'* (UCAS, 2016).

Every year the most common opening line in personal statements is something like: 'From a young age I have been interested in/fascinated by...' So, encourage your son or daughter to open with something personal, relevant and **specific** that **differentiates** them from other applicants.

On the other hand, as some admissions staff have advised, don't try too hard to come up with a killer opening:

- *'Don't waste time trying to think of a catchy opening; it's often a complete turn-off.'*
- *'Your interest in the course is the biggest thing. Start with why you chose it.'*
- *'The best personal statements get to the point quickly.'*
- *'I often advise applicants to start with paragraph two, where you get into why you want to study the course. That's what we're really interested in.'*

Endings can also be tricky. Your son or daughter should conclude with something **specific** that adds to the statement, not something generic that adds nothing significant to what has already been said. That's why 'At university I want to learn more about...' is potentially quite a strong ending whereas 'In conclusion I believe that my passion for business and my strong work ethic make me a perfect candidate for this course' is a weak one.

In fact, 'bigging yourself up' is not a good tactic. Admissions staff want you to **demonstrate** your qualities, not just claim that you have them without providing **evidence**.

## Speak to your referee

That's where the academic reference comes in. It's normally written by teachers and tutors, it has the same 47-line and 4,000-character limit and admissions staff will normally read the statement and reference as one continuous document. And it's here, in the reference, that 'he/she has a strong work ethic' is much more appropriate because it's the teachers confirming it rather than the applicant claiming it.

In fact, a team approach between student and referee can be very effective, because the best references are ones that complement and add something to the personal statement. Three ways to enhance this team approach are for your son or daughter to:

- alert their referee to any important selection criteria that can be evidenced in the reference
- make sure they know about your son or daughter's achievements or what they do outside the classroom
- ask the referee to include in the reference anything your son or daughter doesn't have room for in their statement.

## Finally

There is plenty of constructive and inspirational advice out there, especially on the UCAS website (www.ucas.com), on independent websites like *Which? University (*www.university.which.co.uk) and on some universities' own websites or individual course web pages.

So, for the best results, encourage your son or daughter to:

- do their research
- be themselves
- believe in themselves
- be specific, reflective and enthusiastic
- and let their voice be heard!

Meanwhile, for you as a parent, it's great that you are taking an interest and providing support and, if you spot any obvious mistakes, especially in spelling, grammar or punctuation, do tell them. However, also remember that it's your son or daughter's voice that universities will want to hear, not yours. If an adult has helped them write it, universities can tell!

# Chapter 8

# Clearing made clear

*Gill Sharp*

The purpose of this chapter is to explain how Clearing works and help candidates maximise their choices and avoid common pitfalls during the process.

## What is Clearing?

For the uninitiated, Clearing is the process that takes place in August after A level and equivalent results have been announced. Most students will have applied via UCAS (Universities and Colleges Admissions Service) the previous year and they can hold two offers, one for their first choice course, the other, typically asking for lower marks, as an insurance place. These are both conditional on achieving certain grades. If those sought after results prove elusive, UCAS – the honest broker in the Clearing procedure – aims, like any good matchmaker, to unite universities whose courses are not full with potential students desperately seeking a degree. So far, so simple.

---

**Top tip:** Clearing is not a feeding frenzy, though sometimes it is portrayed as such. So sure and steady trumps fast and furious! It's worth remembering that Clearing doesn't actually close until mid-September, though premium places tend to disappear well before that.

---

## Clearing candidate categories

The largest group are those who have received (ahem) disheartening grades and thus been rejected by both their Firm and Insurance chosen degree courses. But let's not forget those who have done better than expected (yes, it does happen) and can use Clearing to source universities who want high achieving candidates. Of which more anon, under 'Adjustment uncovered'. And there's also scope for those who did not register with UCAS the previous autumn but, buoyed up by better results than anticipated, are applying for the first time. They pay the minimum fee, write a personal statement, arrange a reference, then dive head first into Clearing.

---

**Top tip:** Most, but not all universities take part in Clearing: e.g. Oxford, Cambridge and most but not all of of those institutions sometimes described as 'elite' are notable absentees. But those who think that their grades deserve attention can call the missing institutions and state their case.

---

## The process
1. Early morning of results day: university decisions (not results) published online on automated UCAS Track system
2a. Students not accepted by first choice university allocated, via Track, to insurance choice. Students not accepted by either choice are placed

into Clearing and given their all-important **clearing number**, without which they cannot pass GO.
2b. Students eligible for Adjustment are given reminder of this on Track.
2c. Students with a slight glitch in grades whose application has not yet been declined/accepted need to make a cunning plan (see 'Lost in limbo').
2d. Both these latter groups need to draw up a rationale as to why they merit a place and contact universities direct.
2e. Those who've changed their mind about choice of university see 'This is where it gets complicated' below.
3. Mid-morning: students collect actual exam grades from school/college or through the post.
4. Time for reflection on next steps and exploration of opportunities usually via the UCAS link which collates course vacancies by subject. Short-list the academic opportunities that appeal, pulling together compelling evidence as to why student is a good fit for possible universities.
5. Early to mid-afternoon (times vary each year) Clearing starts. Swing into action, calling the likely universities in order of preference. Keep UCAS correspondence, password, reference number and clearing number to hand. Remember – only a single Clearing place can be selected at a time, so flirt with as many as you like, but commit to just one.
6. Preparation pays off!
6a. university accepts candidate and vice versa, or
6b. university indicates interest – invites student for interview/visit. May ask to see portfolio (for certain creative and technical subjects) or example of course work.
7. The UCAS machine swings into action. Candidates need to keep eyes wide open for further instructions, emails and paper correspondence, all of which have to be dealt with before the place is finally secured. Use the system or lose the place.
8. A switch of plans may mean emotional adjustments: modifying long held ambitions and plans is never easy. On a practical plane, remember to sort out, change or chase up funding arrangements.

**Top tip:** This may be too little, too late, but it's a good idea NOT to be on holiday when the results come out. If it all goes pear shaped then, there are many positives to being near a reliable email and phone connection, not adventuring in the Andes or partying on Paphos.

Much of what this chapter covers, particularly in terms of choosing, and clinching, a place is relevant to all three groups described earlier, but most of all to...

## The disappointed many

Those whose grades didn't cut the mustard. They are not alone, although both they and you may feel very isolated indeed. Most will have been told via UCAS Track that it's thanks, but no thanks. Or they will have received results from the exam board by post or through visiting school/college. There will be tears, tempers, rages, rancour. And that's just the parents. Maybe it's pointless telling you to hold back on clashes over clubbing (too much) and recriminations over revision (too little) or possibly tantrums over teaching (patchy or poor). But if ever there was a time to focus on the future, this is it. You can't put the past to rights – unless maybe you ask for results to be reviewed, of which more later, or there were genuine mitigating circumstances for indifferent grades. In that instance get on to the universities pronto and explain the circumstances. Will they listen? Some will, some won't. But if you don't ask, you don't get.

## Adjustment uncovered: the lucky few

Candidates who have exceeded the grades wanted by their original UCAS choices may feel that they want to capitalise on this and perhaps aim for higher ranking universities or new courses. UCAS Track will flag up those who are eligible and if they want to try their luck elsewhere, they have five days (i.e. five consecutive 24 hour periods including weekends), during which they can contact universities and potentially negotiate another place, secure in the knowledge that their original firm offer will still be waiting for them if those discussions fail.

## Lost in limbo: decision deferred

Where a student has had just a minor glitch with grades, admissions tutors might

- postpone judgement for a few days or

- make a changed course offer which the student is not obliged to accept.

UCAS does not allow universities to keep candidates hanging on indefinitely, but in the first situation, the student can feel that they are in no man's land, compounded by the worry that should the eventual verdict be thumbs down, plum alternatives will already have been gobbled up. In either circumstance, the student can seize the initiative. If they are still keen to secure a place, they might send additional evidence (outstanding assignment, work experience reference, details of voluntary work, extracurricular achievements) that will strengthen their position.

If they would rather be sent to their insurance place or take their chance in Clearing they can ask to be 'released' straight away, as they have not met the original conditions for entry.

---

**Top tip:** Some deferred outcomes are caused by universities waiting for additional exam marks such as GCSE (not published until the following week). Hang on in there with gritted teeth and keep a weather eye on Clearing possibilities in case they are needed further down the line.

---

## Strategy for success

a. A cup of tea and a calm appraisal of the situation.
b. Ask questions: do they still want to go to university – this year, next year, sometime, never? A gap year can clarify career aims, allow time for resits if these are necessary or enable the student to travel/work/stockpile cash. An apprenticeship meshes learning with earning, up to and beyond degree level. You see where I'm going with this – there are other options and they merit serious consideration.
c. If the answer to b. is yes, then more questions follow:

- a new subject? What?
- a different university? Where?
- both the above? Why?

Time spent on unravelling this now will save a lot of doubt and disillusionment further down the line. Snatching at any old random opportunity is not the way to go.

d. The three Rs – in this case research, research, research. The UCAS website has links to all the courses currently available. These are updated regularly (but not in real time). There will be fluctuations over the next few days, but most places, except those in the most popular subjects at the most prestigious universities, will be around for a while. So see what's out there. Make a little list based on responses to c. Then dig deeper. Clearing won't open until the afternoon on results day, so check the online prospectus for a lengthier lowdown and maybe even a virtual campus tour. Does the course seem suitable? Is it what your son/daughter wants? Where does it lead? Read the small print: does your son or daughter have the right grades in the relevant subjects? Location, as we know, is important, but don't discount degrees on those grounds alone – why else were trains and coaches invented?

e. Think and think again. What is your offspring going to say to the admissions tutor? How are they going to defend indifferent grades or market outstanding ones? How will they respond when asked what attracts them to the university/department/degree? Some staff in certain universities won't put you through all of these hoops or indeed any hoops at all. On the other hand, there are many who will probe the rationale relentlessly and ruthlessly. You get one shot at each course. Don't waste it.

---

**Top tip:** Those going for a specific career such as law or psychology should ensure that the degree offered is approved by the relevant professional bodies.

---

## Phone protocol

Tutors want to talk to potential students not their doting or despondent parents, however clued-up or well-meaning. So unless there is some good reason why you have to speak on your child's behalf, just help them prepare. Then make like a butterfly – hover reassuringly and quietly in the background.

Academic issues aside, remember to:

- have clearing number, UCAS reference number, Track password at your fingertips (and ideally to hand)
- verify actual place of study: will it be the main campus or in some far-flung outpost of the university?
- mention the A word – accommodation; lack of suitable housing can be a deal breaker in Clearing
- obtain, note and securely file the name, phone number and email address of everyone you or your child speaks to. You are likely to have to contact them more than once.

## Words from the wise
Careers expert Nick Hynes is a veteran of the national exam results helpline, TV and radio. He says, 'Clearing can be a marvellous second chance at getting into a university course which is right for you. In a typical year, maybe 15% of candidates secure their place this way. But it is not an easy option. You will have to research suitable courses just as thoroughly as when you first applied – and be prepared for some tricky telephone interviews! Think what you might be asked and what you want to say before firing up that phone.'

## This is where it gets complicated
While Clearing itself is essentially a straightforward procedure, there are potential pitfalls, usually born out of misinterpretations and misunderstandings. The most common are:
- that students can accept a place which they don't necessarily want and then switch to something more congenial on arriving at university. Step back! It varies between courses and institutions, but this kind of transfer can be problematic, prolonged or downright impossible: it would be a mistake to bank on this option
- that a student who has met the conditions needed can change their mind about accepting their Firm or Insurance offer and go straight into Clearing, no questions asked. The legal bit: your child effectively signed a contract with the academic institutions concerned. The universities agreed to take them if they made the grade. They are not going to renege on the deal and don't expect the candidate, who made a corresponding commitment to take the place, to do so either. So in order to go into Clearing, students would have to ask to be released from these obligations. If the university agrees, securing their freedom might be a protracted process. It could be up to ten days before a Clearing number can be issued, with no guarantees that alternative courses will still be available.
- so why not simply decline the unwanted place(s)? Bad idea if they are rarin' to go. They would then be cast adrift from the UCAS system until the new cycle begins in late September and they can reapply for the following year.

## Hitting the mark: getting exam grades checked
When results are unexpectedly low, there is a natural tendency to think that getting the papers re-marked (or 'reviewed' to use the official terminology) will provide – hey presto – the magic solution. Sadly, it ain't necessarily so. Of course, some people come out smelling of roses with higher marks and degree places secured. But whisper it softly, results can be downgraded or, as Andrew (see later) discovered, just remain at the same, dispiriting, standard. Nor are universities compelled to keep places open if results are being reviewed:

UCAS encourages this, but as a recommendation not a rule. It's down to individual institutions. It might depend on individual powers of persuasion, so marshal your arguments well.

**Top tip:** Exam boards rarely respond to individual approaches for reviews, so if one seems relevant, your first stop is the school or college which can advise further and, if necessary, appeal on the student's behalf.

## Help at hand

If it all seems overwhelming who can offer assistance?

- some schools and colleges organise careers staff to be in situ on results day, others are closed and shuttered. Best to find out in advance what the arrangements are, to avoid wasted time and ongoing frustration.
- depending on where you live, there may be an independent careers centre in striking distance – and yes, they are open in the school holidays.
- if you still draw a blank, many universities run their own phone helplines which can offer good (but not necessarily impartial) advice.

**Top tip:** For many years there has been a country-wide helpline, running for several weeks over the results period, delivered by experienced careers advisers, like Nick Hynes (see his previous comments). Widely advertised in the press, broadcast and social media, it specialises in objective, pragmatic and informed guidance on next steps.

## Useful websites

UCAS:
www.ucas.com
www.ucas.com/ucas/undergraduate/ucas-undergraduate-apply-and-track

Groundwork on grades required by each university is best done at the Which? University website:
www.university.which.co.uk

## Andrew: a student's story

Strictly speaking, Andrew didn't go through Clearing – but he did have close encounters with many of the situations described thus far. He wanted to study a science degree, but his grades were not as high as anticipated and he and his parents had to recalibrate their expectations. His first choice university, a highly ranked institution, turned him down. He called them and tried to make a case for being accepted, but they weren't budging.

*'They said as I did not get an A in chemistry at least, they could not consider me. Obviously upon receiving results which you believe do not reflect your potential or abilities it is difficult not to feel that you perhaps don't have what it takes to succeed, as does being turned down by a top university.'*

Fortunately, he met the conditions for his insurance course, which was happy to accept him. *'A strong insurance choice allows you to keep your options open and to get to university.'*

Nonetheless, Andrew still hankered after the original choice, so asked his college about contacting the examining board. They send him one of his marked exam papers to look over, and he decided not to go ahead with an appeal.

*'In response to my disappointing grades I chose to defer for a year which is a valuable option. This allowed me to try new things and push myself in different ways before university – for instance studying further in other areas (music), to take a retail job and earn money, and to learn to drive.*

*A gap year has prepared me much more for the rigours of university than I could have possibly done in one summer, including a chance to be reassessed for dyslexia to see how it may have affected my A levels, in order to try and develop new methods of learning to cope with higher education.*

*I cannot overstate how much having a place at university waiting has taken the pressure off my aims for this gap year. This has reflected well on the university application system. However, I do think it is possible some top universities may rely too heavily upon grades and that perhaps they should look more upon the all-round character of a student.'*

## So remember…

Second choice doesn't mean second best!

**Chapter 9**

# First year at university: surviving, thriving and growing a career

*Gill Sharp*

The purpose of this chapter is to identify typical issues and experiences on arrival at university, to resolve common dilemmas and to demonstrate why careers and employability are important from day one.

I know what you're thinking. They have only just finished Highers/A levels/ IB/you name it. Why fret about the future now?

Starting university is a huge catalyst and no-one would begrudge a new student (or fresher in local parlance) a bit of downtime. Students need space to adapt to maybe fleeing the nest, embracing a new lifestyle, and often a new city, making another group of friends, and settling into a different way of learning. However, the three or four years of a degree course pass very quickly and the pace picks up when the first few terms are done and dusted. Once your son or daughter has got their feet on the ground, they need to start thinking about the next move.

---

**Top tip:** No-one is suggesting that they need hurl themselves headfirst into career planning as soon as they arrive on campus, although some – super focused, super confident and super ambitious – do. But career foundations can be put in place incrementally, i.e. in baby steps until a sense of direction becomes clearer. Because the problem with taking your eye off the career ball is that it may mean that your child is (temporarily) relegated to a lower place in the league at the end of the season a.k.a. graduation.

---

First things first. Let's put everything in context and look at what happens when students first arrive at university. Many – perhaps the vast majority – feel excited and elated with their new found status as both a fully-fledged adult and a bona fide student about town. They throw themselves into a new lifestyle with gusto and verve, perhaps overdoing it either in terms of social life or in joining every group, society and event on campus. (Neither stance is recommended.) But moderation eventually prevails and bright eyed enthusiasm may not endure. '*The novelty wears off*,' reports the mother of one fresher. *'In her first few weeks she was euphoric. Loved the lectures, even adored her assignments, bonded (like Bostik) with her new flatmates. But after a while, classes lost their gloss, essays became a bit more of a chore, and flat-sharing revealed its more mundane side.'*

Same old, same old: what was new and stimulating becomes part of an established routine, not to mention throwing up unexpected glitches, such as juggling a busy personal life with the need to put in the hours at the library, lab and lecture theatre. Often even the highest achieving students are flummoxed by the fact that the academic bar is set unexpectedly high and the competition for top marks is tougher than anticipated.

Katie is in her third year now at a well-regarded university in London but can still recall how she felt when starting her course:

*'Everything seemed daunting at first and it was quite a shock to the system. There's so much on offer it can get overwhelming. Making new friends was a sort of saving grace. The lectures were long and I was very tired. My time management was bad too, but it got better when I realised what was expected and that missing hand-in dates led to low marks! Any other surprises? Realising that if I didn't do my own food shopping, no-one would do it for me!'*

**Top tip:** Katie's confusion about the non-existence of a grocery fairy (or indeed its cleaning, cooking or bed-making counterparts) is common. Before you send them off, arm them with basic domestic skills and the ability to make a few meals of the quick, cheap and easy variety or it will be permanent pot noodle territory all the way.

## Confounding great expectations

The majority of students adjust quickly – notwithstanding fleeting bouts of homesickness or lapses in self-confidence. However there are a few who are disappointed, disengaged, down-hearted, downbeat and quite frankly dejected. They may have chosen the wrong subject, course or even university and now feel trapped in the system. Or they might struggle to gel with their new peer group or pressing academic demands. Add to this the usual late teenage insecurities and it can be a case of 'Should I stay or should I go?'

This can be compounded by what we might call the international dimension. Students from Europe or further afield often feel at odds with unfamiliar teaching methods. Combine this with often imperfect language skills, plus the need to adapt to what is essentially a different, some might say alien, culture. One student from China spoke of feeling lost and confused, particularly by the competitive atmosphere. Perhaps international students are necessarily more self-aware than others, because, strangely enough, they are among the first to seek help before a minor disconnect becomes a major issue.

**Top tip:** There are students who enrol at university either reluctantly or on auto pilot, because their school and/or family is insistent that they follow a particular educational route or even a specific degree. So, parents, be careful what you wish for when advising children about which course and career to follow: a disaffected student is not a happy student.

---

Whatever the cause, students who are finding it difficult to cope educationally or emotionally have plenty of help on tap. First port of call may be their own personal tutor and, if additional input is needed, there are whole departments full of professionals ready, willing and able to assist, most neatly wrapped in the banner of Student Services or Student Welfare. These various individuals offer expertise on everything from study skills to finance, via disability, careers, counselling, international students and learning support. If the student decides to remain in situ, ongoing assistance is available. If they elect to leave, they will be guided into the next stage of their journey.

So – worst case scenario – what happens if your child decides to discontinue or, as you may think of it, 'drop out'? Read on for reassurance…

## Drop out or spot on?

Kayl Romain Bailey decided to take computer science at university on the not unreasonable premise that he enjoyed IT and it was a career where he could make money. Six months in, he realised that higher education wasn't necessarily for him at this point (and maybe never) and that he had rather sleepwalked into a degree. Even at such a young age Kayl had a back story of being a successful football coach, and had been much in demand in that capacity for several years. Even when studying, romancing and clubbing also became a very large part of his life, he never let these get in the way of his coaching primary after-school clubs, independent teams and ad hoc one-to-one sessions.

Once he decided to quit university at 18, he expanded his coaching empire, taking on new teams and private clients, as well as state schools. Two years down the line, he runs his own academy and has bought a Merc (yes, really). Happy ending all round and one can only imagine that we shall hear more of him (remember the name).

OK, so Kayl has a marked entrepreneurial streak and would probably have flourished at whatever he set his mind to. Perhaps not every 'discontinuing' story has this fairy tale conclusion, but most have a successful or satisfactory outcome at a level appropriate for the student concerned.

New avenues aside, there is nothing to say that they can't return to their studies: universities are keen to hold on to students with potential, so there is always the possibility of time out and a return to education the following term/year on their original course or some other degree. Transferring to another university is trickier but can be negotiated.

---

**Top tip:** The often unspoken fear of students and/or their parents is that taking time out or switching course will damage any embryonic career prospects. Rest easy: however big a deal it is for those involved, to graduate employers it's just a tiny blip and one that they have come across many times before. Recruiters tend to focus on the here and now and the final outcome rather than any historic hitches.

---

## The careers conundrum

**Myth buster:** there seem to be two campus fables in wide circulation:

- careers advice and events are aimed solely and firmly at those in their final year.
- careers advice is only for people who already know what they want to do.

Bunkum. Baloney. Balderdash. Nothing could be further from the truth: students are welcome in university careers centres at any stage: some would say the earlier the better. As expounded below, there are now also all sorts of careers programmes aimed fairly and squarely at freshers. And if careers services catered just for those who had already decided on the way forward, clients would be thin on the ground indeed.

So that's two myths scotched in one paragraph then.

## Time is on your side?

Ridiculous as it may seem, students hoping to enter the corporate world in any of its shapes and forms need to get their act together very early in the proceedings. Why? Consider this:

- major employers run spring insight programmes and open days around Easter and the early summer of the **first year**,
- longer and more defined placements (holiday internships and vacation schemes) in the **second or penultimate year**, and
- graduate schemes kick into action in the **final year** just when the academic action is hotting up and assignments are coming thick and fast. So students who haven't put in some groundwork earlier in their course are coming from way way behind.

In each case deadlines are from three to nine months ahead: will you do the maths or shall I? Freshers aiming at careers in, for example, law, finance, consulting or accountancy, need to be at least researching, if not making, applications in the autumn term when they first arrive at university. Enough said...

What if your child is not aiming at big business? Does that give them more leeway? Er, no, not necessarily. Where few formal schemes for getting experience exist e.g. in science, in the charity field or in any branch of the wider media and heritage sectors, students are expected to generate these themselves. So, to take just one example, woe betide the would-be journalist who hasn't put in an apprenticeship on the university magazine or undertaken a period of sustained blogging (preferably both and maybe with a placement on a local rag thrown in for good measure).

---

**Top tip:** It's predicted that students graduating over the next few years will typically have three separate careers (and many more jobs) in their professional lives. This may involve various work styles, not necessarily 9-5, nor even just working for one employer at a time. It could also cover entrepreneurship or self-employment. For some, it will mean taking up roles that are currently still in their infancy (vlogger or e-merchandiser, anyone?) or not even dreamed of yet. Just as few in the mid-20$^{th}$ century could have imagined deteriorating demand for (say) bank managers or the existence of possibilities such as web developer or green energy consultant, so the graduate jobseekers of the 2020s and beyond will be exploring uncharted and exciting new territories.

---

## The race is on

At many universities – often those riding high in the league tables – the competition to establish a place on the career ladder is keen, not to say occasionally cut-throat, from the start. With students hustling and jostling early for voluntary opportunities, input into relevant clubs and activities and, especially, entry to employer schemes, a cool head and sharp elbows are needed. Many fellow freshers find this off putting and alarming: one student, six months into an engineering course at a well-regarded university, pronounced it 'toxic'. Another, at an equally well thought-of institution, asked if he *had* to buy in to this frantic frenzy: he wanted to concentrate on his coursework, but was wilting under peer pressure. The answer was if the heat was too intense, stand well back from the flames. If that seem to contradict what has gone before, consider the difference between doing *something* towards your future career at an early stage and *doing everything at once*. The latter is fine for those who have the time and energy, but one size doesn't fit all. The final alternative – doing *nothing* – is less appropriate, even if the student is putting career planning on hold.

## If not now, when?

Without the right foundation in place, a graduate job hunt can be a protracted process. Even those who start early may take six months or more to find employment or further study. Too late to roll up to the careers centre at the end of final year hoping that a job or postgraduate course with your child's name on it will be waiting. Not to mention the fact that if his/her CV is pretty much a blank canvas when it comes to experience and extra-curricular activities, they have even more ground to make up.

---

**Top tip:** Are you thinking that as your offspring will be opting for further study, that takes the pressure off? Think again. Many post-graduate admissions tutors will want to see relevant experience (placements, involvement in relevant campus activities) on application forms and so will prospective employers, who'll be trawling for Masters or diploma candidates as soon as term starts.

---

## Careers and employability: what's the difference?

You may hear the term 'employability' bandied about and wonder exactly what it means, especially as some university careers centres now incorporate the word into their branding.

Put simply, employability is the art of making oneself attractive (and hopefully irresistible) to employers, not only through educational excellence, but also:

- via relevant experience and a professional outlook (exemplified by a sparkling CV, attendance at careers led events and an understanding of what particular jobs involve) and
- a proactive approach to life (as enshrined in involvement in non-academic activities), not to mention
- demonstrating the three Cs: communication (in all its written and verbal forms); collaboration (teamwork/leadership); commercial awareness (understanding that organisations need to make a profit).

## Where does the careers centre come in?

Careers staff aid students with all aspects of investigating career choices, job hunting, employability and opportunity awareness (knowing how to spot a career opening, connection or lead as soon as it comes up – or even before it arises).

Here's a brief menu of what might be on offer for freshers:

- Advice and support for discontinuing students
- Assistance with finding part-time jobs on campus and beyond, and also with temporary summer work
- Access to internships
- Physical, virtual or verbal information
- Opportunities for insight weeks and open days with employers
- Information on volunteering
- Careers fairs, careers talks, seminars, workshops, some offered by employers, some by the university itself
- Opportunities for particular groups of students (e.g. those taking certain subjects or aiming at particular careers)
- Help with diversity and disability issues affecting future employment
- Guidance when exploring post-university options: work, entrepreneurship, time out or more study
- Ditto if considering a change of course or a change of heart about original career plans
- CV and application checks for jobs and courses
- Interview advice (that includes interviews by phone and video – the latter are to here to stay and students seem to find them particularly problematic)
- Networking: an art essential to finding and securing opportunities
- Promoting skills and sourcing opportunities on social media. Your son/daughter may be an ace on Instagram and savvy on Snapchat, but different techniques are needed when it comes to using these platforms (and their professional equivalents such as LinkedIn) to clinch work and internships.

I could go on, but you get the general picture. The list is not exhaustive and will vary from place to place, but gives a flavour of what a student can expect. Of course, some universities go the extra mile and here are just a few examples…

## Early birds and worms

An experienced lecturer at a well-known university's business school realises that *'Employability is not something that features highly on most freshers' 'to-do list'!'* However, she and her colleagues have a programme in place to introduce students to what is expected when they go on placement, and to upgrade CVs that need to go up a notch (or more) from those used for school work experience or for casual jobs. *'By ensuring that all first year students have an up-to-date professional CV and some basic employability training, we give them the tools that enable them to recognise and make use of opportunities with confidence.'*

Another leading university offers something similar to its first-year engineers. The careers consultant co-ordinating the scheme admits that it was not flavour of the month when it began. *'The students couldn't see the point and have since admitted that they hated it – and us.'* But now, a couple of years down the line, with the first participating cohort due to graduate, the students concerned openly acknowledge that it has been hugely beneficial.

A third university has a menu of paid 12-week internships, available on and off campus and open to all students: this enables students to research different job areas in a safe environment and boosts students' confidence and their perceptions of how businesses operate.

There are many more initiatives of this kind for first-year students: ideal introductions to employability – ignore at your peril.

---

**Student standpoint:** Max is from Estonia and studying biomedical engineering at a well-established university. Here is his take on some of the topics covered in this chapter:

*'I started a medical degree back home – mainly my parents idea! I disliked my studies and decided on a complete change of location and subject. I had spent some time in England before, so came and worked in London until the start of a new course, which I am really enjoying. This all made it quite easy to fit in culturally and linguistically. I'm with a group of high achieving ambitious people, so the amount of pressure has come as something of a shock! It took time to realise that although I was always top of the class at home, this wasn't going to happen here.*

*I've taken a part-time job helping out in the careers service: it's raised my business awareness – and will be potentially useful in all sorts of ways in the future!'*

---

**Top tip:** The UK is possibly unique in its attitude to post-university careers which are often open to all, not just those with the 'right' degree. About 40% of jobs at this level are for graduates of any discipline so, to give just two examples, it is perfectly possible for someone with a BA in history to go into finance or a chemist to become a journalist. In other instances there are conversion courses that can turn, for examples, linguists into lawyers and artists into accountants.

---

## The last word
Time flies. Students who start sifting the options and developing experience early are in pole position at graduation. Read more at:

TARGETjobs:
https://targetjobs.co.uk/

Prospects:
www.prospects.ac.uk

**Chapter 10**

# Life's opportunities: how to make the most of them

*Debbie Steel*

This chapter looks at the ways in which your son or daughter can get the most out of life by taking part in all sorts of enrichment activities. Not only will they enjoy themselves, but they will develop skills that will be useful in all aspects of their future lives. Along with gaining work experience (see chapter 14 *Work experience: how to make the most of it*), it'll also help them when it comes to applying for courses, training programmes and jobs.

## What opportunities are there?

Firstly, let's take a look at the wide range of opportunities out there. We've split these into different categories, but some overlap. This isn't an exhaustive list, but it'll give you a flavour of what might be available for (and appealing to) your son or daughter.

### Volunteering

There are lots of ways to volunteer. Here are some examples:

- **community work** – helping at a daycare centre for older people, working on hospital radio, marshalling at a charity race, assisting with a soup run for the homeless, helping with swimming sessions for children with disabilities…
- **raising funds** – working in a charity shop, organising fundraising events, collecting money on flag days, taking part in sponsored activities…
- **campaigning/raising awareness** – helping to build a website for a cause, promoting an organisation through social media, helping with mailshots, manning a stand, getting signatures for a petition…
- **practical/environmental work** – nature conservation, ecological fieldwork, archaeological digs, working on an organic farm…

Some types of volunteering require more of a commitment than others. It could be a one-off event, a regular commitment – say one evening a week – or an intensive project, perhaps during the summer holiday or as part of a gap year.

You'll find that there are lots of opportunities for your son or daughter to volunteer locally or further afield. They could volunteer through their school or college, an organisation they belong to (e.g. Guides or Scouts) or through a charity or voluntary organisation that interests them. They could even organise their own volunteering – perhaps helping out an elderly neighbour with their garden or setting up their own wider community project.

To find out more about what your son or daughter could do, encourage them to enquire at your local volunteer centre/bureau – there's one in most towns and cities. They can also search for suitable opportunities through www.do-it.org.uk, www.volunteeringmatters.org.uk or similar websites. There are also lots of sites aimed at those interested in taking a gap year – a good starting point is www.yearoutgroup.org

### Sport and active leisure activities

There are hundreds of different activities your son or daughter could consider – far too many to list here! They will already be aware of the popular sports offered at their school, but there are others that could inspire them – anything from abseiling to archery.

Some sports involve training with a team or club, others are more solitary but still require dedication and commitment. There may be opportunities to take on positions of responsibility, such as captaining a team or coaching younger participants.

The following websites have lots of ideas on ways in which your son or daughter could get involved in sport and fitness, and links where they can find out more about different sports: www.beinspireduk.org and www.bbc.co.uk/sport/get-inspired

Keeping fit – whether through regular team games or going to the gym – has many benefits for mind, body and soul.

**Performing arts**

Through school, college or local groups, your son or daughter may have an opportunity to:

- learn an instrument
- play in a band or orchestra
- sing in a choir
- join or set up a band
- learn a form of dance
- make films
- join a drama group where they might act or help with back-stage activities – lighting, costumes, even directing!

Some of the above require a lot of dedication and time – this might be intense over a short period of time, e.g. in the lead up to a theatre production, or an on-going commitment to practise and rehearse.

If your son or daughter shows an interest in performing arts, encourage them to find out what's available at their school or college, or in your local area.

---

*'When I started my apprenticeship my employer said that she was impressed that I mentioned in my interview that I played the guitar in a band. She said that this shows that I can work well with other people and that I'm reliable – someone who can be counted on to turn up on time and do my best.'*
Zak, Apprentice hairdresser

**Representing others**

There are various ways in which your son or daughter can represent the views of other people and express their own, such as through:

- standing on a committee, e.g. at their school, college, university or youth club
- being a form captain, house leader, student rep or prefect
- the British Youth Council (www.byc.org.uk) – an organisation that empowers those aged 25 and under to influence the decisions that affect their lives; the Council supports young people to get involved in democracy locally, nationally and even internationally
- standing for election as a Member of the UK Youth Parliament (for those aged 11-18) – find out more at www.ukyouthparliament.org.uk

**Involvement with organised groups and national initiatives**

There are organisations your son or daughter can join where members meet regularly and take part in a range of adventurous and other activities. These include:

- youth clubs
- Girlguiding (www.girlguiding.org.uk) and The Scout Association (www.scouts.org.uk)
- the Army Cadet Force (www.armycadets.com), Air Cadets (www.raf.mod.uk/aircadets) and Sea Cadets (www.sea-cadets.org)
- St John Ambulance (www.sja.org.uk/sja/young-people.aspx) – runs various schemes for young people of different ages for those interested in first aid and other activities.

The **National Citizen Service** offers 15 to 17-year-olds in England a chance to take part in a range of physical challenges and social action projects during school/college holidays – www.ncsyes.co.uk/ncs-for-your-teen

The **Duke of Edinburgh's Award** or DofE (www.dofe.org) is a well-established scheme for young people aged 14-24 to develop their skills through a package of challenges including volunteering and an adventurous expedition. There are three levels: Bronze, Silver and Gold. There may be a DofE centre at your child's school, college, youth club or other local organisation.

---

*'The DofE really helped to develop my daughter's confidence. She enjoyed the different challenges – even hiking and camping – I didn't realise she had it in her!'* Caroline, mother of Emily aged 17

**Young Enterprise** offers a number of different programmes for young people through a network of business advisers linked to schools, colleges and universities. It aims to give young people confidence, skills, support with job applications, and even the chance to set up and run their own business for a year. There's more information at www.young-enterprise.org.uk

### Other ideas

It's impossible in this chapter to mention all the ways young people can enrich their lives, but apart from the ones already mentioned, your son or daughter may find that they would enjoy:

- photography
- participating in a reading group
- collecting – anything from comics to antiques
- travelling – perhaps backpacking in the UK or overseas
- growing vegetables or flowers
- car, motorcycle or bike maintenance
- arts and crafts – sewing, jewellery making, ceramics, stained glass...
- carpentry or metalwork
- learning a new language or improving one they already know
- anything where they can become an enthusiast – from coding to train spotting!

Your son or daughter can get involved in some of the above through self-study – for instance, they could learn from online tutorials, audio materials, apps or distance-learning programmes. They could also consider joining a local group of enthusiasts who meet to share ideas. There are also formal classes – evening, weekend or holiday courses may be available locally, or there may be workshops or private tutors to get them started.

## Helping your son or daughter choose

It would be wonderful to have the time and money to do lots of the things mentioned in this chapter, but realistically, your son or daughter will have to choose between activities. To help them do this, we suggest asking them some searching questions.

- **What really interests you?** They shouldn't choose something just because their friends are doing it.
- **What's your main motivation for considering an activity or interest?** Perhaps they have a particular skill they want to develop, or a cause they want to support.

- **What sort of activity would suit your personality, skills and aptitudes?** If they have lots of energy, for example, they could channel this into a sport.
- **How easy is it to do the activity locally?** They need to think about what's available, when it's available and how they will get there.
- **How much time will be involved?** Although it's important to experience lots of things in life, most young people have to fit activities around their studies or work. It's important that your son or daughter thinks about the commitment involved.
- **How much will it cost?** They need to be realistic. Some leisure pursuits are free or cost very little, whereas others are expensive. There may be equipment to buy, course or membership fees and/or travel expenses. Support may be available with costs and it may be possible to buy second-hand equipment. Some activities offer taster sessions so that your son or daughter can check that they will enjoy something before joining up.
- **What support and supervision will be provided?** You want to give your child freedom but also ensure that they are safe. This is especially important with active leisure pursuits, trips away, overseas volunteering etc.

## The benefits of enrichment activities

Taking part in activities has many benefits; these vary depending on the activity itself, but most give your son or daughter the opportunity to:

- do something enjoyable and productive (you're less likely to hear them say they're bored!)
- have a break from the pressures of everyday life
- expand their outlook, meet new people and make new friends; even with a solitary interest, there are networking opportunities
- improve their self-confidence
- develop some useful employability and life skills – not just the obvious ones (communication, teamwork, independence and so on), but perhaps more specific skills related to the activity itself, such as first aid or digital skills
- find out whether they would be suited to a particular career
- gain experience; for some types of work – archaeology, nursing or social work, for instance – they'll need relevant experience to stand a chance of getting a training place or paid employment in that area
- boost their CV/job applications or UCAS personal statement
- have something positive and interesting to talk about in interviews (and socially!)

- perhaps get a reference or achieve a qualification
- in some cases, be more open-minded, empathetic and respectful
- challenge themselves and get a sense of achievement.

*'I knew I wanted to train as a primary school teacher so took every opportunity I could to work with children. When I was in year 12 I gained an award in coaching swimming and spent the summer helping with classes at my local pool. Along with my work experience, this was another thing I could put on my UCAS personal statement.'* Charlotte, BEd student

**Top tip:** Ask your son or daughter to go through all the benefits listed here in relation to a specific activity. Which apply?

## Getting the most out of their experiences

It's all very well undertaking an interesting activity, but it's important that your son or daughter makes the most of it, particularly when it comes to course and job applications.

Encourage them to consider the following questions in relation to the activity or activities they have experienced:

- What did you learn?
- What skills have you developed?
- Who else was involved?
- How did you manage your time?
- How has it helped you personally?
- How can what you've learned be applied to your studies?
- How can what you've learned be applied to the entry requirements of a course or job?

**Top tip:** When your son or daughter applies for a job, get them to think about one activity they have particularly enjoyed. Ask them to list all the skills they gained from this activity and compare these with the skills required for the vacancy.

## Finally

Even if your son or daughter only gets involved in one activity, it could make a big difference to their lives and their future career. Support them as much as you can by at least alerting them to what's available. It might take a bit of persuasion trying to get some young people off the couch, out of their rooms or away from their digital devices, but it'll be worth it in the long run. And with so much choice, there has to be something to spark their interest.

**Chapter 11**

# The labour market: keeping up with the changes

*Michael Spayne*

This chapter starts by reminding us of the central role that work plays in human life. It then explores some of the factors that are driving change in the labour market. We then look at the direction and nature of that change by highlighting some key factors which should be taken into account when considering future careers. All these things have implications for the jobs we do, how and even where we do them.

## The centrality of work in our lives

Work is a central feature of human culture and personal identity, indeed the philosopher Martin Heidegger claimed that work was **the** central feature of human existence. Many of our surnames are linked to the jobs which our ancestors did; Smith, Taylor, Cooper etc.. When meeting someone for the first time it is usually not long before the question of what you do for a living is raised. On TV quiz shows contestants are invariably introduced by being asked their name, where they are from and what job they do.

The average person in the UK spends 80,000 hours over a lifetime in work. Once more, the rise in average life spans and changes to pensions means that this is likely to increase in future. Indeed young people today are expected to work for longer than any other generation in history.

As well as paying a wage, which helps us to pay our way in life, work brings us many other benefits. These include the opportunity to do something we enjoy and see as worthwhile, the chance to meet other people, and work can also give us a structure and purpose to life.

Work clearly has a massive impact on our life chances. So decisions which affect our careers are amongst the most important and influential choices we can make. And yet the evidence suggests that many people are not happy in their jobs. For example, a recent survey showed that more than half of British workers would rather be in a different career.

This may suggest a lack of planning and forethought. Indeed it has been said that some people spend more time planning their holiday than planning their career.

---

*'The illiterate of the 21st century will not be those who cannot read and write, but those who cannot learn, unlearn, and relearn.'* Alvin Toffler

---

## Looking to the future

The labour market has been transformed in recent times and the pace of change continues to accelerate at, what appears to be, an increasingly fast pace. In this environment, it is often difficult to make sense of what is really going on. And this can create confusion and uncertainty, particularly when comes to making choices for the future.

However, we cannot know what the future holds, uncertainty is part of life. Unexpected things happen and have an impact. For example, the 2008 financial crisis was not expected and yet has had unforeseen and long-term consequence on economies and labour markets around the world.

As individuals we can go through life living each day as it comes and effectively hope for the best. Or we can decide that, despite the uncertainty that surrounds us, we can take a view on the future. Through the choices we make as individuals we can do something to increase the chances that our future goes in a positive direction in terms of where we eventually find ourselves in the world of work.

## Employment change over time

As time passes, the jobs people do and the industries they work in change. Some job areas grow and others decline. For example, just after World War Two there were over a million people working in the UK coal mining industry. However, the last deep coal mine in Britain closed down in 2016, bringing to an end centuries of work in deep coal mining.

Conversely, new sectors and occupations have developed and created jobs. For example, the growth of digital technologies has transformed the world of work and now most jobs require some level of digital skills. Indeed it has been said that many of the jobs that young people will be doing in the future do not yet exist.

However, one thing we can be confident of is that the jobs we do in the future will, in many ways, be different to those that are being done today.

## Drivers of change

There are a number of factors which are driving change in the labour market. If we have a better understanding of some of these factors and the direction of change in the labour market then perhaps we have a better chance of making sense of the labour market and hopefully make better choices. Here we look at three of these key drivers.

### Globalisation

We live in an increasingly globalised economy with large volumes of trade in goods and services taking place between countries. However, labour market(s) are increasingly global too. The World Bank estimates that 250 million people live and are economically active in countries other than where they were born.

In the UK about one in seven people in employment are from overseas. This pattern is repeated to a greater or lesser extent in many of the advanced economies of the world especially those in Western Europe, North America, Australasia and parts of the Middle East.

Job opportunities exist right around the world and many employers are looking for talent globally. Around one in ten of the UK's most qualified and skilled workers have already been tempted to work overseas. Many countries welcome workers from the UK in skill shortage areas. For example, in Australia there are vacancies for motor mechanics, hairdressers and chefs as well as accountants, vets and midwives. All of these are listed as skill shortage areas in that country and well over a million UK citizens currently live and work in Australia.

Those people who are willing and able to be mobile, not just overseas but around the UK too, can potentially have access to a greater number of jobs and career progression opportunities.

---

*'The future always comes too fast and in the wrong order.'* Alvin Toffler

---

## The impact of technology

It is arguably the case that throughout history the development and application of new technologies has had the biggest impact on jobs and perhaps on history itself. This is also true of the rapid pace of change in the labour market of the early 21$^{st}$ century.

Indeed the development, application and spread of technologies proceed at a faster pace than ever before. The world-wide-web was invented in the 1970s and desk-top computers and the internet only became widespread in the 1990s. Yet in a relatively short time these technologies have transformed the way we live and work.

Yet, people have sometimes responded negatively to new technologies, fearing that they would destroy their jobs and livelihoods. For example, the Luddites in the 19$^{th}$ century and the print workers of Wapping in the 1980s.

However, history arguably suggests that the majority of new technologies have created more new jobs than they have destroyed. Indeed technology has seen productivity and standards of living rise significantly in recent generations.

Advances in knowledge and the spread of new technologies, particularly digital technologies, continues to transform the world around us including the world of work. Digital skills are pretty much essential to live and work in modern society. Continued developments in robotics, genetic science, artificial intelligence and many other emerging technologies will arguably have a massive impact on the world of work in the coming years.

Technology probably means that some jobs will disappear and other jobs could be de-skilled. However, technology also creates other jobs including highly-skilled roles in areas such as research and development, production, manufacture, servicing, marketing and sales.

## Towards a low carbon economy

There is, broadly speaking, consensus around the world that the planet is going through a process of climate change brought about by global warming.

Most climatologists believe that this phenomenon is man-made and is primarily caused by burning fossil fuels which release carbon dioxide into the atmosphere. In response, many governments around the world have starting to accelerate their efforts to address the problem.

This includes putting in place policies to encourage a more environmentally sustainable and lower carbon economy. This means that the way we travel, produce energy, manufacture, build, utilise natural resources and dispose of waste is changing. Once more, these changes impact on the type of jobs we do and how we do them.

For example, within the construction sector there has been a trend towards modular building technologies. This means that building components are produced off-site as modular units or 'pods' before being transported and then assembled on-site. As well as a range of environmental, time and energy saving advantages this type of approach also means that a different mixture of skills and occupations are required when compared with more traditional construction methods. For example, using this approach, up to 90% of the 'construction' work takes place off-site, meaning there is less need for traditional building skills on site – such as bricklayers, plumbers, electricians and painters and decorators.

This is just one example of how a move to develop a more environmentally sustainable world is also driving change to the skills and occupational make-up of the construction workforce.

Some people claim that the transition towards low(er) carbon solutions will bring about a green-collar revolution that will help transform our economies, generate new jobs, change the way we perform existing jobs and lead to a more environmentally-sustainable way of life.

## Things to consider
### Spatial concentration of work

One impact of the changing labour market is that some jobs tend to be increasingly clustered into particular geographical areas. For example, Cambridge is home to one of Europe's largest technology hubs, employing 57,000 people across 1,500 businesses. In addition, global cities also act as magnets for human talent. For example, London is a centre for the financial, fashion and media industry, while Dubai attracts many skilled and educated workers from around the world, including over 100,000 from the UK.

The existence of clustering and global cities means that knowledge, skills and jobs often become spatially located in these employment 'hotspots'. Moving from one job to another and career progression is not something that just happens in time, it is something that happens in space too.

This means that geographical mobility is arguably an increasing factor which jobseekers need to take into account as they plan their careers.

## Qualifications and earnings link

The evidence shows that there is (still) a strong link between qualifications and earnings. Employers are prepared to pay higher wages to people who have the qualifications and skills they want. In other words, (on average) people with higher levels of qualification tend to earn more than those with lower qualifications or no qualifications at all.

The difference in lifetime earnings between some occupations can be the equivalent of a lottery win. The potential return on investing in qualifications and skills, in terms of increased earning power, is a factor that should be taken into account when considering future careers.

## What employers want

Despite the labour market being in a constant state of flux, a wide range of research has shown that there are common skills and qualities which employers want from their workers.

These skills and qualities include a need to have good literacy, numeracy and IT skills. However, employers also want workers who are motivated and have a positive attitude at work. These qualities are often referred to as soft skills which are transferable between jobs.

We would not want to give the impression that qualifications are not important to employers. Indeed, qualifications are increasingly required in the modern labour market and many job vacancies do require particular qualifications before you can even apply. But employers are looking for much more than qualifications. Those young people who can demonstrate that they have the skills and qualities which employers want are likely to be more successful in their efforts to find a suitable job.

## Employers' top ten skills

1. Verbal communication
2. Teamwork
3. Commercial awareness
4. Analysing and investigating
5. Initiative/self-motivation
6. Drive
7. Written communication
8. Planning and organising
9. Flexibility
10. Time management.

Source: The Careers and Employability Service at Kent University

## An ageing workforce

The population dynamics of the UK mean that we have an ageing workforce. Many people are living longer and even after, what is for many, a prolonged period in education young people are now effectively being asked to work later in life than their parents and grandparents generation(s).

Indeed the traditional concept of retirement is becoming increasingly obsolete. This means that for an increasing number of people changing careers in their later years and/or taking part in phased retirements (which includes continued participation in work at some level) are expected to become more common.

While these issues may seem a long way off to young people, they do need to be aware of this development and its implications for work, pensions, finances and indeed life-long learning and adaptability.

## New jobs and replacement jobs

The majority of job openings (or vacancies) in the labour market occur because people leave their jobs for one reason or another – for example, to change jobs or retire. When this happens they often (but not always) need to be replaced. This means that we should not just focus on brand new jobs or expanding sectors but also remember that there are often job opportunities in sectors that have been in decline.

For example, the number of civil servants has fallen in recent years, mainly due to cuts in public spending. At face value this might suggest that the Civil Service is not a good place to look for a job. However, because of the number of people retiring from the Civil Service there are still thousands of vacancies each year simply to replace those who leave.

---

*'Change is not merely necessary to life – it is life.'* Alvin Toffler

---

## An increasingly flexible workforce

The traditional full-time 9-5, five day a week job is no longer as dominant as it used to be, as flexible working practices have become more common. There are now more jobs available offering part-time hours or temporary contracts. Many employees are also expected to work shift patterns or during the evenings and weekends. Self-employment and freelance work is also much more common than it used to be.

The concept of the 'gig' economy is increasingly used to denote the growing use of flexible labour including the use of short-term contracts and freelance workers. It has been estimated that five million people, around one in six, of the workforce are employed in the so called gig economy.

This increase in flexibility does mean that many people will have a variety of different jobs throughout working life. While there are some positive elements in this trend, there are some negative implications too. In particular this has contributed to work becoming more precarious in nature.

## Towards an hour-glass shaped labour market

For many years economists have been claiming that we are moving towards a higher skilled and knowledge-based economy which will see an increase in professional and knowledge-based jobs and a decline in lower skilled and lower paying jobs.

However, while the evidence shows that there has been growth in professional, managerial and associate professional jobs there has also been growth in some lower skilled and lower paying jobs too. In addition, it can be argued that lower skilled jobs as a whole have proved to be more resilient than previously expected.

There has also been some decline in middle-tier jobs particularly in skilled craft occupations and in administrative and clerical occupations.

Some have described this (apparent) trend as a move towards an hour-glass shaped economy. And while the picture is perhaps more complex than this, the concept of the hour-glass labour market is still one that, in simple terms, does makes some sense in terms of what is happening. In other words there has been a polarisation of jobs.

## Inequality in the labour market

There is a widespread focus on equality and diversity in modern Britain. However, the reality of the situation is that when we look at the labour market we can see patterns of inequality.

Work and the rewards from work are not shared equally across the population. Some people are fortunate to find themselves in relatively secure and well paid jobs whilst others find themselves in lower paid and more precarious work and may experience frequent spells of unemployment.

The reality of the situation is that worklessness and poor quality jobs are widespread and there are winners and losers in the labour market.

However, those who are better placed to take advantage of education and career opportunities tend to benefit most from the jobs and careers available. We cannot choose to whom and where we were born and these factors do have a big impact on our life chances. However, most of us can arguably make some choices which can make a positive difference to our lives and our careers.

> **Top tip:** If you want your son or daughter to maximise their employability, then they should consider the following: flexibility; adaptability and mobility.
>
> **Flexibility** – many jobs require workers to be flexible. For example, some jobs require shift work or require employees to work evenings or weekends. Others take work on short-term, temporary contracts. These are all examples of workforce flexibility.
>
> **Adaptability** – the jobs which are available and how we do them are constantly changing. Workers need to be able to adapt to this change by being ready to accept new working methods, learn new skills and, when necessary, move to different jobs.
>
> **Mobility** – consider moving away or increasing your travel to work time to get the job you want or to take advantage of education, promotion and career development opportunities.

## Summary

The labour market has been changing at a fast pace in recent years and this pace of change is expected to continue and accelerate in the future. These changes are driven by a myriad of factors including globalisation, the impact of technologies and the move towards a low(er) carbon economy. These drivers of change mean that the jobs we do, and how and where we do them, are changing. These changes have implications for the skills and attributes needed for success in labour market. Being aware of the drivers of change and the implications these have can help us to make more informed decisions regarding our future in the world of work.

**Chapter 12**

# The labour market: how to find the best information for you

## Helen Janota

When the time comes for your son or daughter to seriously start thinking about which career path they might want to pursue, they will want to do as much research as possible. Exploring job or labour market information (LMI) as it's often referred to can be a powerful tool when used carefully but this can seem quite a daunting task – living in the Information Age means we have a vast amount of information at our fingertips and not all of it is what we need. This chapter will help you to discover some of the free resources which can support your son or daughter's decision making and their school may also provide access to other, useful careers resources.

Young people today are facing a more complex and competitive labour market than you, their parents, will have experienced. You'll have high hopes for their futures including their future careers and as well as learning about the world of work in school, for those hungry for more information, they can begin to explore LMI for themselves.

Knowing what the labour market wants – such as what employers are looking for in an employee – will allow your son or daughter to develop the skills, attitudes and qualities that they need to travel along a pathway towards their dream job. The previous chapter *The labour market: keeping up with the changes* explains what the labour market is like and some of the general trends your son or daughter can expect to see in their lifetime; this chapter suggests ways in which they can explore jobs and careers further to help with their decision making.

By using some of the recommended tools in this chapter, your son or daughter can begin to gain insight into careers they might be interested in, but to make sure that they have fully understood the information, it's always a good idea to discuss their findings with an expert careers adviser. Getting to grips with what some of the data really means can be a little bit tricky!

---

**Top tip**: Suggest that your son or daughter discusses any labour market information they think is relevant to the career they are considering with a qualified careers adviser.

---

Your son or daughter will most likely be asked to think about what their likes and dislikes are in terms of the type of work they might want to do and to consider which school subjects they enjoy or excel at when thinking about future careers. As well as understanding themselves, they also need to know what the realities of the labour market are so that their aims are realistic and achievable. This means the full range of jobs available to them (locally and beyond) and how they can prepare themselves for success.

---

*'In recent years I have noticed an increase in young people asking questions specifically related to LMI. For example, I am often asked about future prospects within a specific industry, the best location for finding work, and help understanding the different entry routes into careers. As a careers adviser I rely on accurate, reliable, and up-to-date LMI to help guide young people with their career planning'.* Katherine Jennick, careers adviser

## What is labour market information?

In a nutshell, LMI is the facts and figures about the jobs and vacancies employers have and what they want from an employee.

These include:

- average earnings
- qualifications and skills requirements
- predicted trends for jobs and sectors
- the key sectors in an area.

LMI also includes information on the workforce, or people who are looking for work, such as:

- the types of jobs people are in
- whether people are in full- or part-time jobs
- people's qualification levels
- how a job is split between males and females
- the number of people who are unemployed.

## What kind of labour market information is useful to young people?

Your son or daughter doesn't need to know everything about the labour market but referring to high quality information is key to gaining an accurate picture. Try to steer them away from using Google or another search engine when researching careers – the information they find will only be useful if it's up to date and relevant and it's not always obvious. With the whole of the internet available at the click of a button, it's difficult to know if something is from another country, out-of-date, inaccurate or biased.

---

*'In my work with year 11 students it is really important to use LMI to be able to help them develop their awareness. Lots of their ideas are based on very limited knowledge about what jobs exist; these are often jobs they come across in everyday life or know about from TV such as teachers, social workers, solicitors. Without developing their knowledge of the labour market young people are limiting themselves and not choosing from all the potential careers that could excite them!'* Jackie Pickles, careers adviser

---

Below are some of the areas your son or daughter might want to look for when researching their potential future career.

## Average earnings

Pay can vary across regions – someone in London will most likely be paid more than someone doing the same job in the East of England. Looking for regional or even local earnings can help your son or daughter get a realistic picture of what they might be able to earn in their chosen career.

Comparing the pay between different jobs can also be a useful exercise. The more qualifications your son or daughter has, the more their earning potential will grow. Seeing in black and white that an engineering technician earns more than a factory operative or that an events organiser could earn more than a travel agent can be a real motivator!

Most websites that show a range of job profiles will give average earnings and some, such as the Careerometer tool for England (see useful websites at the end of this chapter), allow you to compare the average salaries of a range of jobs side by side.

## The characteristics of particular jobs

This might include typical weekly hours worked, what percentage of people in that job are full-time, part-time or self-employed and what proportion are male or female.

Knowing this information can help your son or daughter build up a picture of what the realities of working in particular job might be like. For example, 75% of people who work as waiting staff are in part-time roles. It's true that some will be working part time through choice but it will also be the case that not all jobs will offer full-time hours.

And don't let the fact that some jobs are made up of largely male or female workers put your son or daughter off that career. These industries are usually desperate to create a more diverse workforce and are crying out for women or men to join, as well as people from a variety of backgrounds.

Websites such as www.icould.com and www.startprofile.com give a breakdown of workforce characteristics such as these.

## Qualifications, skills and attitudes

Knowing what employers want and expect is probably the most useful piece of labour market information your son or daughter will need. How else will they know which qualifications to aim for or which skills to develop to secure an interview?

While you can get a good indication of which skills and qualifications are a priority for specific jobs on a number of websites such as national careers services, UCAS and Start (see the end of the chapter for web addresses), some company websites will give tips and advice for applying.

If you want to help your son or daughter explore their skills there are some good free resources such as Barclays Lifeskills and Start.

## The different pathways into a job

Young people have more options available to them in terms of training and qualification routes than previous generations. Improvements to the quality of apprenticeships – more employers are involved in their content – have increased the variety of routes into lot of jobs and switching between vocational and academic routes is now much easier too.

## Predicted future trends

We can't know for definite what will happen in the future but by looking at data from previous years and looking ahead to advances in technology and shifts in the ways we live our lives, experts can make predictions around what is likely to happen.

The previous chapter *The labour market: keeping up with the changes* gives an overview of how we expect work to change but we can also view predicted trends for specific jobs on many of the careers websites highlighted at the end of this chapter.

Take care when looking at any charts as scales will vary. Some jobs may look like they are on the decline but look more closely at the numbers and it may be by just a handful of jobs. It's also worth talking to your son or daughter about replacement jobs: some areas of work may not be creating lots of new roles but they may expect to see hundreds of workers retire in the near future and will need young people to replace them.

## What the job is really like

It can be hard for young people who have had little experience of the world of work to get a realistic picture of what a particular job is really like. A work experience placement or part-time job, while extremely valuable, usually only gives insight into work in one sector. Job profiles are available on most careers websites (see the useful websites listing at the end of this chapter) and some websites, such as icould and Careersbox, offer a wide range of videos of people talking about the jobs they do and how they got there. Usually, these profiles will also give a link to industry websites where more detailed information, including LMI, can be found.

**Top tip**: Listening to people talk about their experiences of work, and how they ended up where they are now, can be motivating and inspirational.

## The competition for jobs

If you've seen stories in the news about hundreds of people applying for a single job then you'll know that some jobs are highly sought after. In cases like these, the successful applicant will have exactly what the employer is looking for.

Researching sector LMI is key to finding out how that particular industry is faring. You can gain industry insights and learn more about which jobs are experiencing skills shortages and which have high competition.

Is your son or daughter set on working in a particular sector? LMI can help them to discover the roles where there are skills shortages. The film and TV industry, for example, is a popular choice with young people. Typically, vacancies for production assistants or presenters will attract plenty of candidates but some of the more technical roles such as camera technician are struggling to attract people with the right skills. It might be that by pursuing a slightly different career to the one they were initially considering they may get their foot in the door of that desired sector more easily than another. Again, a chat with a careers adviser will help them to explore their options.

**Quick fact**: Employers across all sectors are struggling to find people with the right skills for some roles – these are often referred to as skills shortage roles.

## Local jobs

One of the recent criticisms of careers education in schools is that students are finishing their education without a clear understanding of what the labour market wants. And this couldn't be more important when it comes to local priorities.

In all areas of any country some jobs will always be present. There will be vacancies for doctors, nurses, retail assistants, refuse collectors and chefs in all local areas – day to day living couldn't carry on without them! But some jobs – especially knowledge intensive, creative and highly skilled roles – can appear in clusters, with some areas having many more opportunities than others. Examples include biosciences, motorsport and gaming.

So each local area has different key sectors with particular needs and for them to thrive, grow and keep providing jobs, local employers need the local workforce to have the right skills to fill the vacancies as they arise.

A website such as Start (www.startprofile.com) shows the availability of particular jobs in a region – a great start for a young person wanting to know their potential options in a specific geographical area. For those who don't shy away from data, the UK government's Nomis website (www.nomisweb.co.uk) has a wealth of information on the labour market. You can view the figures for people working locally in particular sectors right down to district level and even compare them with previous years.

Another way of finding out what's going on locally is to use live vacancy boards such as Adzuna (www.adzuna.co.uk). This has some really useful information on local labour markets based on the number of vacancies posted. For those who like their information in graphics, the vacancies map is a really useful tool!

The UK government's 'Find an apprenticeship' service can also be used to research apprenticeship opportunities in different areas. Simply narrow or widen a search or choose different towns to view the number of vacancies currently on offer, then use them to build up a picture. The number of vacancies may vary at different times of the year – lots of employers open their apprenticeship programmes around the beginning of the year.

It's important for your son and daughter to be realistic about their chosen career path – researching the local labour market will help them to understand whether the career they want to pursue offers enough opportunities if they want to stay in their local area. If it might not, they may need to consider commuting for work or even relocating.

## Work may keep on changing but advice is on hand

High-quality LMI is more important than ever because the jobs landscape is changing at a rapid pace. Some LMI can be hard to navigate and it's always a good idea for young people to ask for the support of a careers adviser who will have the expertise to help them make sense of the changing world of work and its demands. But freely available information as discussed in this chapter, when we know it is reliable, can really make a difference to those who are making those all-important first steps in researching the careers that await them.

## Useful websites

National Careers Service (England):
www.nationalcareersservice.direct.gov.uk

NI Careers Service (Northern Ireland):
www.nidirect.gov.uk/campaigns/careers

My World of Work (Scotland):
www.myworldofwork.co.uk

Careers Wales:
www.careerswales.com

Start:
www.startprofile.com

icould:
www.icould.com

UCAS Explore jobs:
www.ucas.com/ucas/after-gcses/find-career-ideas/explore-jobs

What Do Graduates Do?:
https://luminate.prospects.ac.uk/what-do-graduates-do

Careerometer (LMI for All):
www.movingonmagazine.co.uk/careerometer

Nomis:
www.nomisweb.co.uk (for those who like looking at numbers)

Find an Apprenticeship:
www.gov.uk/apply-apprenticeship

Barclays Lifeskills:
www.barclayslifeskills.com

Adzuna:
www.adzuna.co.uk

Health Careers:
www.healthcareers.nhs.uk

Go Construct:
www.goconstruct.org

Tasty Careers:
www.tastycareers.org.uk

Tomorrow Engineers:
www.tomorrowsengineers.org.uk

Lantra (land-based careers):
www.lantra.co.uk

For more sector-based information, recommended websites often appear at the end of job profiles.

# Chapter 13

## Application forms made simple

*Ellie Stevenson*

An application form can be a crucial early step on the journey to getting a job. This chapter will show how your son or daughter can make their form the best it can be, and how you can help.

> '*On application forms, I'm looking for experience, but for a first job you don't always get that. So then I'm asking, what do you do that's service, that serves people? It might be volunteering, community work or the Duke of Edinburgh's Award. I'm also looking for passion, enthusiasm.*' Jane Webb, retail operational manager

While many employers still rely on CVs and a covering letter, some organisations prefer to use their own application form. An employer may use an application form rather than a CV and covering letter because it allows them to:

- get the answers to the questions they want
- compare the responses of different candidates easily.

Many sections on the form are standard, but your son or daughter should always tailor their form to the job, especially when completing the personal statement (the section where they can sell themselves to the employer and show what they have to offer). A form may be available online or on paper, depending on the company but if completing a paper application form, applicants should use a **black pen** and CAPITAL LETTERS, unless the form specifies otherwise.

If your son or daughter would benefit from this, you can set aside time to help them with filling in their online or paper form.

Even if not, every form should be proofread and checked for grammar and spelling. A parent or carer can be a great help in this regard – a fresh eye is always useful! If you do, read the form as if you were the employer, not a parent.

A copy should be kept, and if the form is an online one, printing a copy of the form **before** submitting (if possible) can make it easier to check. Errors can be easier to spot on paper than on screen.

## Online forms

Over the last few years there has been a steady increase in the use of the online application form, which is often completed via the employer's website.

Online forms come in different formats and can be tricky, in that the format can sometimes determine what content is included and how it's displayed, e.g. requiring months as well as years for employment experience.

Your son or daughter should prepare the information in advance as a Word document, particularly the personal statement. The data can then be copied and pasted into the form, although your child will need to check formatting afterwards, and if there is a word count limit, ensure all the content is there.

Preparing the information beforehand means your child will also have a copy which they can amend for future applications if necessary.

To complete an online form, the applicant usually has to register or create an account first (e.g. provide email address and password). This means they don't have to complete the form in one go. It's important to save the information added frequently in case the internet connection fails and your child is logged out.

When using an online form it's advisable to become familiar with the way that particular form works, so for example, can the applicant go back to previous sections? How is work saved? etc.

## Selection criteria

For most jobs there is a job description and person specification. The job description highlights the key tasks and responsibilities of the job, the person specification focuses on the skills and experience and personal qualities required to do the job effectively. These can be designated **essential** or **desirable**.

Your son or daughter's task is to demonstrate that they have all the essential requirements and ideally some of the desirable ones too.

## Preparation

Before completing the application form there are a number of things your son or daughter needs to do.

Research the company, the sector and the job. Parents and carers can be of great help here, making suggestions and helping with research.

Study the job description and person specification. Encourage your child to read these in detail and think about ways they can demonstrate they have the skills, experience or qualities listed on the person specification, giving examples of tasks or activities that demonstrate this.

For example: *'Essential criteria – good verbal communication skills'*

Here your child's response might be something like: I've worked in a sports shop for the last two years, serving customers and helping them choose sportswear. Excellent customer service is very important and I enjoy assisting people and working on the till.

Before preparing the material to include, your child should gather together all the information they'll need, e.g. about their education and qualifications, their job or work experience history and details of referees.

When applying for a job, applicants need to demonstrate enthusiasm, personality and confidence as well as relevant skills and experience. For many young people, selling themselves can be difficult, especially when they might not have much experience.

Encourage your son or daughter to be confident and highlight the **relevant** skills and experience they do have. Remember, a successful form will most likely lead to an interview, where they will have to live up to the form, so they need to be positive **and** honest.

As a parent or carer it's natural to want to help as much as possible. But don't write the application for them. A form will sound more natural if the young person uses their own words.

You can help by making sure they know when the deadline is, and stick to it!

## Typical sections on a form
### Personal details
As well as name and address, your son or daughter should make sure a contact phone number and/or email address is provided. This is especially important if the company wants to invite your child for interview. An email address should sound neutral or professional, not silly or too personal.

### Education
Applicants should always provide the information asked for, but sometimes it's appropriate to summarise, e.g. '5 GCSEs at grade C/4 or above including English language and maths', if a student has higher-level qualifications. Employers will be particularly interested in key qualifications such as English and maths and those subjects/qualifications which are relevant to the post.

If your son or daughter's education and qualifications were gained abroad, they may, for higher-level jobs, need to state the UK equivalent. The Universities and Colleges Admissions Service (UCAS) has information on the comparability of international qualifications and UK NARIC (the designated UK national agency for the recognition and comparison of international qualifications and skills) can provide a Statement of Comparability for a fee.

### Training/Skills
Some forms will ask for information on training or additional skills gained, for example, experience of a particular software package, keyboarding skills, joinery skills, etc. Formal qualifications would normally go under the education section but any additional courses or certificates (usually short or part-time courses, evening classes, or work-related training) can be included here. Only those courses which are relevant to the post or demonstrate a particular skill, e.g. leadership, should be included.

**Work experience or employment history**
In this section your child needs to list their employment history (usually starting with the current or most recent post), describing the main tasks and responsibilities in each role. They should emphasise those most closely related to the job applied for.

When your son/daughter is starting out, there may not be much to put here, but weekend and vacation work, voluntary work, Duke of Edinburgh's Award experience and work experience can be included. Emphasise experience that relates to the job applied for, e.g. *'used MS Office including Word and Excel on a regular basis'*, for a clerical position.

Be sure to explain any gaps in employment history, focusing on the gains, e.g. taking a year off to travel around Asia, meeting a variety of people and building self-reliance and confidence. Similarly, regarding leaving a job – give a brief but positive explanation, e.g. progressing to next post; making a career change.

**Competency-based questions**
These are more frequently seen at the interview stage but some graduate application forms ask such questions. They relate to specific examples of times when the applicant has demonstrated the skills required for a role.

Such questions often seek evidence of skills such as teamwork, problem solving, organisational ability, using initiative and so on.

The **STARR** method is a good way to answer competency questions.

    S – describes the **situation**
    T – what the **task** or target was
    A – what **action** the applicant took
    R – the **result**
    R – **reflection**: not always used, but can be an opportunity for the applicant to show how they reflected on what happened and how they would deal with the situation next time.

When answering competency questions, the applicant should write in the first person, give specific facts where possible (e.g. increased sales by 20%) and end on a positive note (reflection can be used here to show how something could be done better if necessary).

**So, for example:**
*Describe a time when you dealt with a customer complaint* (the employer wants to see if the applicant can communicate effectively, diffuse potential conflict and maintain customer satisfaction).

*A customer complained because she couldn't find the fruit she needed for a dinner party dessert recipe* (situation).

*It was my task to show her where it was but when I checked there was none on the shelves* (task).

*I checked in the stockroom but there was none there either so I suggested our other store, but she had already tried there. I then talked to her about what she was making and suggested other possible fruit options and some ready-made alternatives* (action).

*The customer chose one of our ready-made options, and was pleased because we'd saved her preparation time. I also showed her how she could get a discount on the product which saved her money* (result).

## Strengths and weaknesses

Your child may complete an application form which asks about their strengths and weaknesses. They should avoid one-word answers. For strengths, they can give examples of relevant situations, e.g. *I enjoy working with computers in my spare time, and was able to get our office PC working again when it lost power, saving on downtime.*

Weaknesses – your child can think of these as areas for development. They can also look at aspects of their personality. You, as the parent may be able to help with this. So, for example, if they are outgoing, they may have a tendency to speak before thinking things through.

## Interests or activities

The form might not ask about these, but if it does, your son or daughter should pay attention to the skills required by the job and relate interests to these, if possible. So, for example if the job requires visual or artistic skills, mentioning an interest in drawing, photography or working with photos on a computer might be relevant.

Leisure activities can also demonstrate an ability to work well with others, e.g. someone who enjoys reading might wish to highlight that they belong to a book group.

## Personal statement

This section can also be called the supporting statement, supporting information or additional information. It is, in many ways, the most important part of the application and gives your child the chance to sell themselves to the employer. The key points they should cover are:

- why they want the job and why they want to work for that particular company (this can sometimes be asked in a separate section, rather than as part of the personal statement)

Your son or daughter's answer should stress what they can do for the organisation. As a parent or carer you can help them identify what they can offer the employer, and why this job in particular appeals to them, e.g. did they study any relevant subjects, or do any similar work experience or role? Encourage your child to think widely about work experience, subjects studied at school and voluntary and other activities.

They should represent the opportunity they are applying for as a chance to gain additional skills or experience, or to develop their career, rather than a wish to leave a current situation, for example, due to bad pay or treatment. Always avoid negative comments on an application form.

The second part of this section of the form should highlight to the employer:

- what they have to offer

and should take up most of the personal statement. It should be answered in relation to the person specification, i.e. how they meet the criteria for the role, ensuring each point on the specification is addressed. **Employers often select candidates for interview based on how well they can demonstrate they meet the person specification.**

Your child should highlight the relevant skills and experience gained in a particular situation, e.g. *I worked for nine months as a retail assistant, gaining valuable customer service experience as well as skills in stock management and control.*

Communication and IT skills are required for many positions.

While it's important to cover all the points, your son or daughter shouldn't write too much. Less can be more in this section.

They should make sure they don't make claims they can't prove, and if possible back up a statement with evidence (e.g. *thanks to my suggestion, sales increased by 20%*).

### The catch-all question

Sometimes, there can be a question on a form which asks for 'Any other information'.

There's no requirement to complete this but it gives your son or daughter an opportunity to highlight other relevant information.

As a parent or carer, you can encourage your child to think of any leisure or other activities that might be relevant, e.g. volunteering, Duke of Edinburgh's Award, school projects or activities, clubs and societies (if not already mentioned).

## CV

There is sometimes the option to include a CV (Curriculum Vitae) **along with** the application form. If one is included:

1. it should be up to date
2. the information should be consistent with that on the form
3. it should add something to the application
4. make sure your son or daughter doesn't leave information off the form because it's on the CV. All relevant information should be **on the form**, which is the main source of information for the employer.

They shouldn't send a CV if one isn't asked for.

## References

Usually a minimum of two are needed.

Most forms ask for a reference from a current or most recent employer and at least one other person.

If your son or daughter is a recent graduate, one reference can be from a lecturer at their university; a personal tutor is a good example.

If your child is a school leaver, they can include a teacher who can comment on their school work and general attitude, and someone connected with any work experience or voluntary/community work they're involved in. Referees shouldn't be family members or related to the applicant.

Applicants should ask the referees' permission **before** providing their details and keep them informed about applications. When time has passed, the referees' details and agreement should be checked as they may have changed jobs or job title.

Your son or daughter should choose referees who can comment positively and relevantly on their experience or skills/attributes.

If your child is applying for a job and doesn't want their current employer to know, they should tick the relevant box/es in the referees section. If there isn't this option, they can ask on the form that a particular referee isn't contacted before an interview or job offer is made.

## Equal opportunity monitoring questions

Most forms have standard questions relating to age, ethnicity, gender, disability and sexual orientation, often on the last page of the form or online document.

This information is used for monitoring the employer's commitment to equality and diversity. It shouldn't be seen by the people involved in recruiting for the role or used in the selection process.

Your son or daughter doesn't always have to answer all of these questions, there's sometimes a 'prefer not to say' option. You can discuss this with your child and help them think about what they want to share.

---

**Top tips:** Your son or daughter should:

- always be honest. Recruiters are adept at spotting inconsistencies/exaggeration and your child could lose their job if incorrect information is discovered later
- read the questions carefully and answer them – answers should be brief and focused and paragraphs short. Make sure they don't repeat themselves
- ensure their language is positive – the application is about the experience they do have, not what they haven't done yet
- only mention information they feel confident speaking about at interview
- where appropriate, use power verbs such as achieved and organised, and descriptive words like effective, consistent and adaptable
- complete all sections of the form – if part of it isn't relevant, put N/A or not applicable
- if taking material from a previous form or notes, ensure it doesn't include references to the former application or employer
- treat an online form as the equivalent of a printed one. They shouldn't use abbreviations, text-speak or language they might use in an email to a friend
- check the dates to ensure there aren't any gaps in education and work history. If there are, a positive explanation is better than leaving a gap, e.g. took six months out to care for an older relative
- be wary of spellcheckers. They can be used, but with care. For applications to UK companies, avoid introducing US spellings such as center
- make sure they've attached any requested documents such as a personal statement or CV
- **NOT** include a photo unless specifically asked for, which should only be where relevant, for example, acting or modelling
- **NOT** leave the form to the last minute, as this is more likely to lead to mistakes and incomplete information. With online forms, system downtime or failure could prevent the form being submitted in time. If it's an online application, once submitted, your child should receive an email confirmation

- keep a copy of the information or print out the form, as this can be referred to before an interview, or can act as a source of reference for future applications.

## Useful websites

Duke of Edinburgh's Award:
www.dofe.org

National Careers Service – how to fill in application forms:
www.nationalcareersservice.direct.gov.uk/get-a-job/application-forms

National Citizen Service parents' page:
www.ncsyes.co.uk/ncs-for-your-teen

UK NARIC:
www.naric.org.uk/naric

Volunteering – the Prospects website which is aimed at graduates but carries some useful information of interest to a wider audience:
www.prospects.ac.uk/jobs-and-work-experience/work-experience-and-internships/volunteering

**Chapter 14**

# Work experience: how to make the most of it

*Susanne Christian*

Some young people choose to do a work experience placement (or several), others have it forced on them reluctantly by their school or college. Whether your son or daughter is allocated a placement or has to fix it up on their own, you can help them think ahead and plan their work experience to get the most out of it – and then use it to get that uni place, apprenticeship or job.

## What's work experience for?

Employers often complain that when young people start work, they know very little about the workplace, business or how organisations work. Work experience (WE) tries to address this by placing young people in a controlled situation in a workplace, usually for a week or two. Employers are very keen to see that applicants for jobs and/or graduate schemes can show they have 'commercial awareness' i.e. knowledge and experience of the business world. Nowadays, of course, this applies to all sectors: local authorities, government departments and the NHS all have to be business-minded.

WE can take place at different times in a young person's education including during:

- year 10
- year 11
- sixth form/year 12
- college courses
- undergraduate courses.

An individual young person may end up doing more than one WE, depending on the courses they choose and the policy of their school or college.

If your son or daughter has no clear career ideas yet, WE can help them decide what kind of work they want to do – or even what they don't want to do! For some people work experience shows them a job which they didn't know about or didn't know they'd enjoy.

---

### Gareth changed his career plans after his work experience

*'I really wanted to go into engineering so I wanted work experience that was something to do with engineering. The teacher told me that placements in engineering are hard to find and offered me retail – in a music store for two weeks. I was disappointed but I thought I'd give it a go.*

*'I loved it! The best thing was being with adults. I know a bit about music so I enjoyed talking to the customers. We'd have some good discussions. It was busy. I didn't mind that, it's better to be busy. I've seen how retail can be a good career. I'd like to be a store manager and see my store achieve the top sales figures.*

*'Now I'm at college on a retail course and I've applied for a part-time job back at the record shop.'*

---

## How to arrange a placement

Arrangements differ. You probably know by now how your daughter or son's school or college goes about WE. Some allocate placements for the whole year group – or use a local organisation to do this, working on behalf of the school/college. Others provide names and addresses to contact.

Most schools and colleges allow young people (or their parents) to organise their own placement. There's nothing wrong with using your own contacts, too, through family, friends or anyone you know who works in the relevant field. It's worth chasing up any lead.

If you have a particular organisation in mind because it fits a career choice, then you can approach them yourself (or encourage and support your son or daughter to do this). You'll be helping them develop networking skills which will be useful in their university and working life.

Arranging their own WE placement could be a definite plus point for personal statements and for interviews. There is a world of difference between 'I did a work placement at XYZ Ltd' and 'I arranged my work placement at XYZ by approaching a senior partner'. Seeing this on an application demonstrates enthusiasm and initiative.

## Plan ahead

If you and/or your son or daughter are arranging their WE placement yourself, this is something to bear in mind:

---

**Top tip:** START EARLY! One thing at least is certain: the process will take much longer than you think.

---

If a miracle occurs and you get a WE placement fixed up relatively quickly and easily, so much the better. You and your son or daughter will have plenty of time to think about and prepare for their WE.

## Looking for a placement

You may have to help your daughter or son do some serious research (another good skill for the future!). Like most information, it's there on the internet. Below are some examples:

- Anything health-related: the NHS Choices website www.nhs.uk lists all NHS services in England (and can redirect you to the sites for other parts of the UK).
- Companies' and organisations' own websites: many large organisations

have their own WE programmes with details on the company website (sometimes in a separate 'careers' or 'work for us' section). **These schemes are very competitive and often have early closing dates so start looking in good time.**
- Professional bodies: most career areas now have a professional body or trade association. These can be a useful source of contacts and some even have web pages about work experience. You can find an alphabetical list of many professional bodies (comprehensive but not exhaustive) at www.gov.uk/government/publications/professional-bodies-approved-for-tax-relief-list-3/approved-professional-organisations-and-learned-societies Many bodies have an education or careers department which could offer advice. **Please note, though, that professional bodies DO NOT arrange placements – you, or your son or daughter, will have to do the donkey-work.**

## Think laterally

If you and your son or daughter are having difficulty in finding something that seems 'relevant', try being a bit creative with your thinking. If your son or daughter is already interested in a particular career, they'll want to use their WE to find out more. Take pharmacy, for example. For a future pharmacist, experience in any part of the process would be useful, including:

- research
- manufacturing
- packaging
- selling/marketing
- prescribing
- dispensing.

And, of course, pharmacists themselves work in:

- retail shops (including many supermarkets)
- hospitals
- pharma companies.

So there could be more avenues to explore than you first thought, especially if it means you can use your personal contacts.

The same goes, of course, for other professions. Fashion, for example, involves design, manufacturing, marketing, branding, distribution and retail.

## If you don't get the placement you want

What if your son or daughter is really disappointed with their placement? Your daughter wanted lab work and she's got two weeks in a local shop or your son wanted outdoor work and he's stuck in an office?

You're probably disappointed for them too. You might even share their feeling that it's a week or two wasted. But as a parent, you can encourage them to think of it as valuable experience.

### Making the best of it

Remind your child that there is much more to work than the operational content of the job. It can be these other factors which make the difference between enjoying a job and just tolerating it because you need the money.

Any workplace will give a young person experience of all sorts of aspects of the world of work, which most of us probably take for granted – and forget that we had to learn them in the early days of our working life.

Most placements will show what it's like to:

- work to targets
- rely on other team members and have them rely on you
- give a hand with any tasks which needs doing
- be supervised in your job
- work for a good (or bad!) manager
- be involved in making sure the business makes a profit
- keep customers happy.

All of which are of vital importance to any organisation – and would give your son or daughter plenty of topics to discuss at interviews or present as a case study at an assessment day.

---

**Top tip:** REMEMBER – any experience is GOOD experience.

---

Help your son or daughter look on the bright side – if nothing else, it's two weeks when they don't have to go to school!

### During work experience

Young people (and parents) sometimes worry that WE will be two weeks of making the tea, photocopying or even just doing nothing. But most employers are well-prepared and have arranged a programme for their WE students, which might include moving round different departments, meetings with managers or site visits (it depends on the business, of course). Many employers encourage WE students to experience real work situations.

### Karam had two valuable placements in year 12

'I thought that it was really important to get some work experience – partly so that I was sure in my own mind that this was what I wanted to do and partly to convince universities that I had done my research.

'My careers adviser helped me arrange the placements. At the international engineering and construction group I spent time seeing how important IT support is to a company, learned how companies tender for business and shadowed a health and safety officer. Another work experience student and I were given a real project to evaluate and report on.

'At an engineering consultancy I shadowed engineers in the drainage and sewerage department and did some calculations and flow rates for them. I also accompanied engineers on visits. One was to negotiate with a farmer who thought that a new main sewer line was going to be too near his buildings.'

Encourage your son or daughter to think about what they'd like to get out of their placement, especially if it links into their course subjects and/or career ideas. They may want to, for example:

- talk to a new entrant to the organisation (graduate or school leaver)
- visit a particular department or see a specific process in action
- discuss with HR what would help their entry into the company or job area.

## Work shadowing

A WE placement usually involves the young person getting involved in the job. But there are many work settings where this wouldn't be practicable – an operating theatre, a court or in the cab of a high-speed train amongst others. Work shadowing is a way for students to get a flavour of a job which they can't do hands on. What they can do, though, is observe.

This might make shadowing sound boring or of little use, but it need not be. The young person can ask questions. The person being shadowed will normally take time to explain what they are doing and why – and allow the young person to be involved as much as possible. Students have successfully shadowed, for example:

- Members of Parliament – who have allowed them to sit in on meetings and surgeries for constituents
- solicitors – who have taken them to observe the workings of a court
- business managers – who have shown them the day-to day running of the business.

(In any profession, sitting in on client discussions has to be with the client's consent.)

Work shadowing typically involves spending half a day or a day with someone. There is no reason why a young person couldn't have more than one shadowing experience, as long as they – or you! – are prepared to fix it up. If shadowing feels like second best, this could encourage your son or daughter to think about it in a more positive light. After all, their peers who are doing a conventional WE placement are spending a week or two in the same organisation so a series of work shadowing days could provide wider experience across the world of work.

## How important is work experience or shadowing?

There are some jobs that are almost impossible to enter without some relevant work experience or shadowing. This is because they are particularly demanding, either physically, mentally or both. The admissions staff and recruiters for these professions want to know that students who apply have a very clear idea about what's involved. Spending time shadowing also shows a real commitment to the work.

Examples include:

- agriculture
- social work
- teaching
- medicine
- dentistry
- veterinary work
- health care professions, such as physiotherapy and occupational therapy.

There is no reason why you can't 'mix and match'.

**Ari's different placements contributed to her career decision-making**
*'I learned different things on each placement and gradually I realised that I wanted to be a doctor. I worked in a pharmacy for a week and enjoyed learning about the different drugs but I realised that I wanted a career with patient contact. I would have liked to spend longer than a day in the GP surgery, but it was difficult for the practice as they had to contact every patient who was due in that day and get their permission to have me present.*

*'In my week's work experience on a hospital ward, I wasn't allowed to do very much because I hadn't been taught any basic nursing skills but I developed a role for myself doing whatever needed to be done that I was capable of, and spent a lot of time talking to the patients. I was allowed to observe several procedures too. One was a heart scan. We had just started to study the heart in biology, so it tied in really well with my academic work, but I didn't know very much. When the doctor asked me how many valves there were I got the answer wrong!'*

## Using work experience

Many young people think of using their WE placement for their UCAS statement. Their experience can also help with material for:

- uni interviews – especially if something on their placement really made them decide 'this is the subject I want to study'
- Apprenticeship interviews – employers will be glad to hear that a young person knows something about the company or job they are applying for
- assessment centre case studies – where they may be asked to talk about how a particular business operates
- job interviews – answering questions about working in a team, using communication skills, problem solving, planning, etc.

Although employers are interested in what WE a young person has done, they are far more interested in what they made of it and how it has shaped them – and how they put this across during the application process. In personal statements (whether for UCAS or other applications), where space or word count is limited, it can be more effective to mention a particularly decisive moment than speak generally about the whole placement. Employers and university admissions staff all want applicants to show enthusiasm.

Incidentally, there are other possible ways that your son or daughter may be able to use their WE in future:

- their two weeks WE in a shop may help them get a weekend job to help them through college or uni
- when they finish uni, your son or daughter may not move straight into a graduate-level job. Their WE might be useful for that 'stopgap' job

## Internships

A quick word about internships. There is no standard definition to distinguish 'work experience' from 'internship'. They both have the same aim – to give an inexperienced young person some contact with a particular career field.

Internships are usually undertaken when the young person is older – after leaving school or graduating – once they know which career they want to pursue. Internships are often longer than school or college work experience – they can be over weeks or months, sometimes full-time, others part-time (one or more days a week).

Internships have attracted controversy, being described as exploitative. The law is clear that anyone performing the role of a worker (with set hours, duties or responsibilities) should receive at least the National Minimum Wage.

## Useful websites

NHS Choices:
www.nhs.uk

Professional bodies and associations:
www.gov.uk/government/publications/professional-bodies-approved-for-tax-relief-list-3/approved-professional-organisations-and-learned-societies

**Chapter 15**

# 'What happens if it all goes wrong?' A philosophy for careers

## Chris Targett

You may be supporting your son or daughter through their career planning while in education or they may be older, having tried out some of the available options but feeling stuck or lost. Wherever they are in their journey through life, this chapter sets out to demystify what might be happening for them and why it might be happening; seeking to answer questions they may ask, such as:

- I'm in sixth form, shouldn't I really know what I am doing by now?
- How do I figure out what I want from life... where should I start?

These types of questions are sometimes seen as the 'big questions' and can be a little daunting for them and us. Drawing on ideas found from within the world of careers guidance, we will aim to help answer these and similar questions. It will provide you with some answers as well as useful tips which will hopefully help you to understand the life stages your child is going through, enabling you to support them more fully.

## What's it all about?

Life is a funny old business, with 'career' just one facet of a much more complex whole. Depending on your belief system, culture and in some countries even class or caste, the idea of what a 'career' may look like or even mean, will differ wildly. Understanding that we all have a different relationship to the concept helps us to appreciate that each of us differs with regard to what we think it can be. Some commentators have mentioned that the very idea of a 'career' is a purely western or middle class concept; one contemporary commentator and respected academic, Gideon Arulmani, talks about the importance of not superimposing our own (western centric) values onto other cultures and that our approach to supporting our children in their 'careers' should reflect the culture or mixture of cultures we are within. See www.thepromisefoundation.org/career-and-livelihood-planning

As a careers adviser I have worked with a wide variety of students who have a diverse range of cultural influences affecting the context of their decision making. Some find their parents are dictating to them what they must choose, such as 'something from the professions' (e.g. law, medicine, dentistry and similar) whereas others have free rein to choose whatever they wish. Some are under pressure to 'choose something which pays' due to necessity, fulfilling immediate needs (other than those of job or career satisfaction). For others there is pressure to follow the family business e.g. 'construction is what we do in our family, so you will too'. All these influences mix with those of teachers and their peers, causing a heady mix for anyone who finds themselves within such a melting pot. Some cope well and others less so, finding the various, well-intentioned advice difficult to square with their own hopes, dreams or desires for the future. It is our role as parents/carers and advisers to help students make sense of what can, at times, seem senseless.

Students can find themselves lost and confused for a variety of reasons, from floundering within a sea of mixed messages, to not understanding what is possible with their next steps after school or later in life. Confusion as to why their ideas have changed as they have got older is common; we see students who at fifteen felt certain of their future direction, hit eighteen and become far less certain; causing uncertainty and sometimes distress. At times, they can feel as if they have made a series of 'wrong decisions' or may have 'failed' their grades and thereby feel trapped by circumstances, with no way out. Through all of this, young people can find themselves feeling all at sea; with often the behaviour on the surface masking their real worries and concerns.

Within this maelstrom there also exists the whims of chaos and an unpredictable labour market which can make potential fools of any who plan too tightly. This combination of external economic factors, influences from friends, family and culture as well as our own internal drivers can best be summed up by the adventurer and writer Kira Salak:

*'We are all at the mercy of a whole slew of forces that are more easily ignored than faced. Forces out of childhood, forces from present causes and conditions, forces as enigmatic as life itself, that tell us we must try to achieve something or get somewhere. No expedition, no journey, no personal challenge seems a product of whim or accident, initiated because something is simply 'there'.'* Kira Salak – *The Cruellest Journey: Six Hundred Miles to Timbuktu*

## So how can we help?

It is useful to have some understanding of what is going on and have some tools to put any concerns into perspective. Developmental theories of career management teach us that we go through different phases in life as we develop our careers, from the 'fantasy' stage through to an 'explorative' and then later 'establishment' stage. Change happens and 'not knowing' as we tentatively develop or try out our career ideas is normal. Recent exponents of this theory however, cite how in the 21$^{st}$ century where it is likely we will have more than one job, we will more than likely cycle round the 'exploration and establishment' stages, as the circumstances in which we find ourselves change. Those who are exploring the effect of automation go further and state how many of us may even have multiple jobs; flux becoming the constant, as we harness our employability or transferable skills in multiple contexts, see www.entrepreneur.com/article/278769

Donald Super, one of the leading thinkers within this area, is a useful reference point if you wish to discover more. See www.careers.govt.nz/resources/career-practice/career-theory-models/supers-theory/

For our young person who may not know what they wish to do at aged 12 or even 17, it normalises their situation. What we know is that when students are faced with education choices at about 13 years old, they are just breaking out of a 'fantasy' stage and entering a period of their lives that may last until they are nearer their 30s (the 'exploration stage') where they are trying things out. It is this we can hold onto and can use to support our young person.

For example, if they find themselves in post-16 education and do not know what they wish to do or be, we can reassure them that it is a very normal thing to 'not know'. Encourage them and help them to try things out (as part of an explorative experience). For those who feel they have 'failed', these experiences can be reframed as lessons.

I clearly remember a student who said she had 'failed' by dropping out of a course at college as she hated it. On reflection, she realised that it was better to learn this now than in two years' time!

Learning what they like and dislike is important and takes time; things do 'go wrong' and can be messy, before they go right. See: www.theguardian.com/education/2016/nov/03/im-an-a-level-drop-out-but-it-didnt-stop-me-from-going-to-uni

We must kill off this idea that those who are successful, succeed first time at everything or know their destiny from the start and then work towards it (such circumstances are incredibly rare). What happens for many of us is that we try things out and through doing so, begin to figure out what feels right for us.

---

**Top tip:** Many students find themselves 'frozen' by uncertainty or expectation and find moving forward or trying anything at all difficult. Sometimes it feels much safer to hide away and try nothing, as nothing is then risked or lost... yet in turn, nothing is gained. Much like with theories of organisational change. See: www.study.com/academy/lesson/lewins-3-stage-model-of-change-unfreezing-changing-refreezing.html.

Students often require moving from being 'frozen' to a point of 'fluidity', where they can try things out and in doing so, discover who they wish to be or could be.

---

Approaches which can help here are those which help them to understand why the current situation of doing nothing is not possible indefinitely and why trying anything is useful. It is these conversations though, which can be the hardest.

---

**Top tip:**

- Ask your son or daughter to make a list or mind map of everything they definitely wouldn't do.
- Now ask them to make a list of everything else that is possible (really think outside the box).
- Identify which one(s) seem the most interesting to them.
- Together, find out if there is anyone in their network (such as parents of friends) or your network who could help provide some work shadowing or experience in these areas of possibility.
- Find out if there are any talks or events which are happening that they can attend, so they can see if there is an interest.

• Book these in and/or arrange... take action!

---

Often independent careers advisers in the community, schools, colleges or universities will also have a list of career-related events or be able to tell you how to access them in your area.

If your son or daughter is having difficulty coming up with a list of jobs or activities they would or would not be interested in doing, there are many online careers tools which may help them build this list. Some schools have software in school which can do this, but there are a number of free resources which can help such as:

- www.startprofile.com
- www.icould.com/buzz
- www.prospects.ac.uk/planner
- www.yearoutgroup.org
- www.seasonworkers.com
- www.do-it.org

Some include 'trait and factor' or personality assessments which can help in identifying areas to try. It is worth keeping in mind that these are dependent on what students input; from experience, they work for some students but not others (there are more complex psychometrics assessments available but usually at a cost).

## Experiencing life

What we can see from developmental theories is that taking the pressure off can be highly beneficial. Reassure your son or daughter that often we have to try out many things before we find the area/s where we wish to be. Sometimes we may find that we wish to do more than one thing, or be more than one thing in life; consider the accomplished sailor Dame Ellen MacArthur who has moved from sailing to successful business leader. See: www.ellenmacarthur.com

Most young people do not really know if their chosen career or job (often idealised before they actually try it) is what they really wish to do. I have seen some students fall into the trap of talking themselves into a certain route. Sadly they can then be trapped by this, as to not follow the path they have talked about for so long would be to lose face; it is then pride mixed with a sense of guilt which eats them up.

Creating a culture at home or school where it is OK to change your mind can be incredibly beneficial in forming a safe 'explorative' environment.

Alongside this, looking for opportunities to try new things and test out ideas can be vital as, in doing so, they can discover what they wish to spend more time doing or being.

Trying things out can take many forms, from courses within education, to taking a gap year, pursing a hobby, volunteering or shadowing someone at work. Such experiential modes of learning sit alongside our formative years where we are also figuring out what type of adults we wish to become and building the skills we need to get on in life. See: www.bbc.co.uk/news/magazine-24173194 If we think back to our own youth, many of us will remember the relationship disasters we had and the fashion faux pas we made; yet we learnt from them. Career learning is the same, as we learn from what seem to be our mistakes and errors of judgements. Often we try things out and they are not what they seem or as we imagined. How we build on these errors of judgement is the crucial part; if we don't reflect and learn, we are then at risk of repeating the same mistakes again.

As parents and carers we need to give our children room to make their own mistakes, encourage them to reflect on what they have learnt from their experiences and then move on. Of course, we do know that for some young people, they do discover what they wish to do, or be, very early on and this does not change; as with all things, there are 'exceptions to the rule'.

For me, it was my good friend Simon who was the exception. I went to primary and secondary school with him and from an early age (about twelve), I can remember him saying he wished to be a 'computer games designer'. Being the children we were, my friends and I laughed and joked with him that it wouldn't happen. Years later through his study, dogged determination and commitment, he became a computer programmer for a leading games company... thereby proving us all wrong.

It is this flipside which shows us that there is always someone else having a different journey through their career. For me, I had to try out a myriad of different things whereas for Simon, he knew from a young age what he would do. For those who do not know though, or whose ideas have changed and have become stuck, being able to move on can feel like a mountain to climb or an impossible barrier to face.

## How to move on

Moving on can sometimes feel hard for our children and frustrating for us, as we can sometimes feel powerless to help and no end of supportive conversations can break the cycle. Finding that our son or daughter is stuck can leave us feeling unsure of how to support them. It is important to remember that even if they have failed all their qualifications there are always options (as described in other chapters in this publication).

At such times accessing independent careers guidance can be helpful, but sadly fully trained advisers are not available everywhere, so having a way to help is important. A tried and tested structure of support is the DOTS model, which was developed by two leading academics. See: www.hihohiho.com/memory/cafdots.pdf Although not perfect for all situations, it can lead you through a series of instructive explorations.

**DOTS** stands for **Decision Learning, Opportunity Awareness, Transition Learning** and **Self-Awareness**; once you rearrange the letters to **SODT** you have a useful sequence of steps you can follow:

**Self-Awareness** – help them to work out what they want from life and career. What is important to them at this stage? Build a list of essential and desirable positions, goals or outcomes. For example, some people 'work to live' and others, 'live to work'. My wife, for many years has seen work as a way to buy equipment for her kite-surfing so, when seeking graduate jobs she was less interested in what she was doing and more interested in what she was earning. For me, I always wanted a job I would enjoy. I spent many years 'trying out' different jobs and in doing so, learnt what motivated and interested me (and what did not). Having an awareness of our own individual values affected the strategies we each took with our careers.

**Opportunity Awareness** – this is all about knowing what is possible and available to you in your situation. It could include knowing about work, hobbies and volunteering as well as an awareness of the local, national and global labour markets. It includes understanding what is out there and how the entry and exit points work, as well as sifting through marketing material and misinformation to identify the accurate information and facts. This can be done using some of the websites and resources listed, as well as through activities such as work experience and visits to schools, colleges, training centres and universities as appropriate.

**Decision Making** – once the above has been explored, deciding what this means to the individual is next. In theory, the more you know about yourself and what you are prepared to strive for (or accept) and, the more you know about what feels possible for you, the more easily a decision can be made and a course charted. However, reflecting on and coming to this decision can take time and the danger is that we fall into procrastination until an external force (such as necessity) forces our hand!

**Transition Planning** – once you know what you want, it is important to work out what you need to do to get there. Some people swear by SMART targets. See: www.bbc.co.uk/education/guides/zxd9j6f/revision/2 while others plan by mind maps or making lists; encourage your son or daughter to use an approach which they have found successful in the past. Imposing your own approach does not mean that this will work for them. I had friends at college who excelled by just leaping and taking a chance when deciding to do something. I had others who planned their revision and essays meticulously, and others who pulled essays out of the bag when the pressure kicked in at the last minute; what worked for one didn't work for another.

## Pre-emptive support

An ideal situation would be for our children to avoid any 'big mistakes' before they happen, but this is seldom possible. We know from our own experiences that sometimes we each have to make our own mistakes to be able to learn from them and that these 'lessons from life' are often useful. Yet some mistakes can be avoided with a little due care and diligence.

Some students drop out of university because they did not check what it would really be like before they started; the same is true for many choices in life. Many of the ideas explored above will help if students are 'stuck', but the same strategies can also help them to avoid these situations in the first place; if they:

- research and check all the facts
- experience the area/s of interest before deciding
- are curious, see www.careers.govt.nz/resources/career-practice/career-theory-models/krumboltzs-theory/

It is often an open mind and curiosity which can be the most effective remedy. If you need further help, there are careers professionals whose calling is to help those in need. Contact your local authority and they should be able to put you in contact with your nearest independent careers service.

# Chapter 16

# Career myth busting: common career misconceptions

*Elaine Mead*

## The six myths you're probably still hearing about careers and youth employment

The internet is a tangled web of information, resources, research and dubious statistics, especially when it comes to the world of careers, degrees and youth employment. It can be really tricky deciphering fact from fiction.

Add to that the personal opinions we all have about young people and careers, based on our own experiences or those we've heard from others, and the trickiness of deciding what to tell your teenagers about getting work ready thickens.

Reports in the media don't always provide a balanced picture, so it's important to make sure you're reading information from different sources, and engaging with accredited careers professionals who can give you the best guidance and build a more accurate picture.

Below we've reviewed the top six myths you might still be hearing, and even thinking, when it comes to careers, and examined them in a bit more detail to give you a more balanced opinion.

## Myth one: If you get a 2:2 in your degree, you'll never get a graduate job

This one has been hanging around the rumour mill for a while, and it's time to dispel it! There are still some very strongly held opinions around achieving a 2:2 (second class honours, lower division), but contrary to popular belief, a 2:2 result is not the end of the world – or career prospects.

### The truth bit
Some high profile employers and organisations will include a first class or 2:1 (upper second class) degree classification as a minimum requirement when applying for their graduate programs. These programs are usually exceptionally competitive, with the employers focusing on taking on the highest achievers to work with, and build a career within the organisation.

### The myth bit
If your child has secured a 2:2, it can be easy to feel as though securing work overall will be a challenge when looking through the requirements of many of these graduate programs. But a grade is only part of the picture, increasingly employers are citing other measures of success or achievement as more important than degree grades. Many organisations have no grade requirements when it comes to graduate recruitment, and there are still plenty of opportunities for students with a 2:2 to launch a highly successful career path, no matter what industry they're seeking to move into.

## Conclusion

Degree grades are only one part of the bigger employment puzzle for graduates. Yes, some high profile companies want the high achievers, but young people with lower degree classifications need to ask whether these organisations would be the most suitable environment for them? More often than not, the answer is no. Being successful as a graduate requires more than some digits on your CV; confidence and support feeds into this too. A graduate with a well-rounded CV of experience, volunteering and extra activities alongside a 2:2 degree will stand out far more than someone with a first class degree but an empty CV.

## Myth two: Doing an arts-based degree is a bad choice for future employment opportunities

Somewhere down the line, arts got a bad reputation in the world of education. It has been bumped so far down the curriculum, it's almost non-existent. We're looking at the future of automation in the workplace and assuming there's no place for the arts. This is not the case.

### The truth bit

The truth is there are a number of graduate jobs and careers that will require a specific subject, or a subject within a related discipline e.g. thinking along the lines of science- and engineering-based roles that will want a degree related to a mathematical or science subject. There are very few career paths that call for a specific, non-vocational arts-based subject, such as English or history.

### The myth bit

That being said, there are still a number of career paths that are open to graduates of any subject. Alongside this, there are plenty of careers that offer conversion courses for those with a good degree qualification (a first or upper second usually). Going back to our first myth on this, the field of accountancy is great example to use here. A graduate with a 2:1 in English who can articulate why they want to pursue a career in accounting is likely to be viewed more favourably than a student with a third class honours degree in economics.

When we think more broadly about the skills and attributes employers tell us they want from new graduates – critical thinking, creativity, adaptability, to name a few – these are all qualities that an arts-based degree lends itself to very well.

### Conclusion

Arts-based degrees still have a lot to offer in the graduate employment market. If you think your teenager has the right attitude and aptitude to achieve academic success in an arts subject, it's a great starting point for a wide number of career paths. If they're unsure what they want to do, pursuing an arts interest is a better starting point than a taking a more technical subject and only achieving mediocre grades, because they weren't that interested to begin with.

## Myth three: There's a perfect job for every student

The idea of securing a job in your twenties and sticking with it until you retire is one of the biggest career myths out there. The Future Workplace *Multiple Generations @ Work* survey of 1,189 employees found that 90% of millennials expect to stay in their job for less than three years. That means the average person would have between 15-20 jobs by the time they retire.

### The truth bit

Some students have a clear idea of what they want to do for work, and that's great! Encourage them to explore their idea through connecting with professionals in the industry, finding out about industry open days they can attend, and speak with your local school's career leader around what other support there is for them to help get them on their way. The earlier they can start exploring the idea, the better set they'll be to make decisions in the future around pursuing this career path.

### The myth bit

For many of us, there really is no such thing as the 'perfect' job. Students shouldn't feel pressured to make these decisions before they're ready, and have had the chance to explore a few different avenues. There is such a thing as a **great** job however; something where your child can feel of value, utilise their strengths and contribute positively. Rather than encouraging your child to pick one career or job title, help them try out lots of different career-related activities that can help them build an idea of what they enjoy doing, and just as importantly, don't enjoy doing.

### Conclusion

Keeping in mind that your child is likely to switch careers a number of times over their lifetime, pursuing the idea of the 'perfect' job seems unattainable. By helping your child to develop a solid foundation of their strengths, their passions, their dislikes, and a sense of purpose when it comes to work, will help them to find not just **one** great job, but multiple different great career paths.

## Myth four: Vocational qualifications provide a much better chance of getting employment than any other qualification

When we refer to vocational qualifications, we mean education routes that typically involve an apprenticeship or studying at a vocational (you may know it as technical) college, but there is also the distinction between vocational degrees and academic or research-based degrees. A vocational degree refers to courses that have a very defined career goal at the end of it – such as medicine, dentistry and engineering.

### The truth bit
It is true, when looking at the research and statistics, that vocational qualifications do tend to offer a more consistent employment outcome than, say, a humanities degree. The Higher Education Statistics Agency consistently places medicine and engineering in the top ten best subjects for new graduate and apprenticeship employment. The more regulated the industry, the more matched education and career paths seem to be.

### The myth bit
Many students hold unrealistic expectations around vocational qualifications. While some expect that completing such a qualification will stand them on good ground for developing the skills they need to secure work once they graduate, there is much more to it than this. Employers want young recruits who have a robust understanding of the career they're going into, and that requires more than an educational certificate. Employers are impressed by candidates who have put in the hard work and effort to secure work experience and placements that support their studies and chosen career – vocational or not.

There are also many vocational careers that do not require a degree to get a foot on the ladder, and where candidates can start developing their in-work skills alongside their studies from the get-go. With the increasing advancement of Degree Apprenticeships, there are many more considerations around this myth than there used to be.

### Conclusion
While a vocational qualification can lead to stronger employment opportunities, this is not the only factor that needs to be weighed up when considering what path is right for your child. It's worth researching the entry level recruitment stats on a course-by-course basis, especially when it comes to vocational courses, and speaking with course advisers around what other development is offered to support students into their chosen career field.

A traditional degree path may not be the absolute best option for your child either. If they are feeling confident and keen to get on in the world of work, the Degree Apprenticeship route could be a great option where they can get the best of both worlds – academically and professionally.

## Myth five: Doing a degree is better than doing an Apprenticeship

It's a question that many careers professionals are faced with. Which is better – a degree or an Apprenticeship? There really is no clear cut, wrong or right answer. Deciding which one is better comes down to the individual young person, where they feel they are at academically and professionally, and which they feel they might benefit from the most.

### The truth bit

There is no real 'truth' that a degree is better than an apprenticeship. The advantage of degrees is that they are readily identifiable as a higher education qualification. Many employers will be readily aware of what having a degree means when young people are applying for roles and graduate programs. When it comes to apprenticeships, defining what your qualification level means in terms of traditional degree qualifications can be harder.

### The myth bit

There is no such thing as one size fits all when it comes to education, and higher education is no different. When weighing up the choice between an apprenticeship or traditional degree path, there are many considerations to take into account.

Degree Apprenticeships are becoming more popular and accessible and, as they offer the same level 6 qualification as a traditional degree path, they should not be dismissed entirely. Apprenticeships typically train and educate you for one specific role or industry, and therefore can offer much less flexibility than traditional degrees. That said, young people who have a definite career in mind could be well placed to take advantage of these debt-free routes. Some career paths state that you must have a degree – particularly those in the healthcare and science sectors – so making sure your child is aware of what the long-term career path requires is another important consideration.

See chapter 6 *Apprenticeships explained* for more information on apprenticeship career routes.

### Conclusion

Deciding which route to follow is a very individual decision, and one that needs to be made carefully, considering all the options. Degrees are not for everyone, and neither are apprenticeships. You can be a huge support for your child when they're looking at their options by helping them explore what's available and letting them know that they have your support no matter what route they decide to take.

## Myth six: The average salary for a new graduate is £30,000

The average graduate salary is a figure that fluxes depending on where you're looking and who you're talking to. It seems that nearly every year different reports provide a different figure, usually without a great deal of context. It's worth keeping a few things in mind when reviewing graduate salaries.

### The truth bit

There are some organisations that do offer higher salaries as part of their graduate programs. These are typically employers who have very competitive recruitment for their graduate roles, and stipulate more stringent application requirements. The *Destinations of Leavers from Higher Education* survey provides a comprehensive review of graduate employment, including graduate salaries. By tracking the career trajectories of leavers in 2012/2013 for five years, they are able to build a robust picture of what graduate recruitment looks like across a realistic time frame. The top end of their results showed that around 11% of the 107,340 respondents were earning £30,000 in 2016/2017 – four years after they graduated.

### The myth bit

While other reports such as those from The Graduate Market and the Association of Graduate Recruiters tend to report higher salaries for recent graduates, the truth is the salaries are very mixed. The *Destination of Leavers from Higher Education Survey* found that the highest percentage of graduates were earning within the range of £25-27,000, but this still only accounted for 14% of respondents. Many graduates were earning between £15-20,000, a perfectly respectable salary. When reviewing reports, it's important to take into account the respondent size, what sectors were contacted, when the respondents graduated and the location of graduates. Local labour markets and economies will all have an impact on graduate salaries, and often those earning in the higher salary brackets aren't necessarily in graduate-orientated roles, but have worked their way up within an organisation they may have been with for some time.

### Conclusion

Keep an open mind when it comes to looking at graduate salaries. Review graduate salaries based on location and discipline, rather than looking at bigger reports that don't drill down into specific data that could actually be relevant for your child. Everyone has to start somewhere, and by doing the right research, you can really help to manage your child's expectations and support them as they start out on their career path.

**Chapter 17**

# careercomp@nion for the journey: useful websites to explore

## NATIONAL CAREERS SERVICES

National Careers Service – England
https://nationalcareersservice.direct.gov.uk

Careers Service Northern Ireland
www.nidirect.gov.uk/campaigns/careers

Careers Wales
www.careerswales.com/en/

My World of Work – Scotland
www.myworldofwork.co.uk/parents

Guernsey
www.careers.gg

Isle of Man
www.gov.im

Jersey
www.gov.je/Working/Careers/

## INTERNET GEMS

### Career Films
https://icould.com

### Job Profiles

Explore careers
https://nationalcareers.service.gov.uk/

Prospects – graduates
www.prospects.ac.uk/job-profiles

What do Graduates Do?
https://luminate.prospects.ac.uk/what-do-graduates-do?

## BUSINESS and FINANCE

### Administration, Business and Office Work

Admin and Clerical
https://nationalcareers.service.gov.uk/

Civil Service Careers
www.civil-service-careers.gov.uk

Local Government Association
www.local.gov.uk/about/what-local-government

Management and Planning
www.careers-in-business.com/management/

Public Relations
www.cipr.co.uk

## Computing and IT

Games Industry
www.screenskills.com/screen-industries/games/

Tech Partnership Degrees
www.tpdegrees.com

## Financial Services

Accountancy and Banking
www.prospects.ac.uk/jobs-and-work-experience

Accounting Technicians
www.aat.org.uk

Careers in Procurement
www.cips.org

Starting out in Insurance
www.rsagroup.com/careers/starting-out/

StatsLife
www.statslife.org.uk

## Transport and Logistics

Air Traffic Controllers
www.nats.aero/careers/

Becoming a Pilot
www.balpa.org/Becoming-a-pilot

Careers at Sea
www.careersatsea.org

Logistics and Transport
https://ciltuk.org.uk/Careers

Marine Industry
www.britishmarine.co.uk/Careers

Network Rail
www.networkrail.co.uk/careers/

Passenger Transport
www.careersthatmove.co.uk

## CREATIVE and MEDIA

### Design, Arts and Crafts

Animation
www.screenskills.com/screen-industries/animation/

Craft Journeys
www.craftscouncil.org.uk

Creative Careers
https://ccskills.org.uk/careers

Fashion Design
www.prospects.ac.uk/job-profiles/fashion-designer

Interior Design
https://biid.org.uk

New Design Talent
www.designcouncil.org.uk

Theatre Design
www.theatredesign.org.uk/

### Gaming and Multimedia

ScreenSkills – Games
www.screenskills.com/screen-industries/games/

ScreenSkills – VFX
www.screenskills.com/screen-industries/vfx-immersive/

Tech Future
www.tpdegrees.com/

## Marketing and Advertising

Advertising and Marketing
www.cim.co.uk/qualifications/get-into-marketing/

Adverting, Marketing & PR Careers
www.allaboutcareers.com/careers/industry/advertising-marketing-pr

## Media, Print and Publishing

4Talent Careers
https://careers.channel4.com/4talent

BBC Careers
www.bbc.co.uk/careers

BBC Careers in Radio
www.bbc.co.uk/careers/what-we-do/radio

Careers in Journalism
www.nctj.com/want-to-be-a-journalist

ScreenSkills – Film
www.screenskills.com/screen-industries/film/

ScreenSkills – TV
www.screenskills.com/screen-industries/television/

StartinTV
www.startintv.com/

Work in Publishing
www.publishers.org.uk/activities/careers/

# CULTURAL and POLITICAL

## Teaching

Further Education
www.feadvice.org.uk

Get into Teaching
https://getintoteaching.education.gov.uk

Maria Montessori
www.mariamontessori.org

TeachFirst
www.teachfirst.org.uk

## Languages, Information and Culture

Become an archaeologist
http://new.archaeologyuk.org

Careers in Conservation
https://icon.org.uk/what-is-conservation

Careers in Museums
www.museumsassociation.org/workforce

Heritage Careers
https://ccskills.org.uk/careers/advice/

Starting your Career – Libraries
https://archive.cilip.org.uk/cilip/

The Linguist
www.ciol.org.uk/news/a-life-with-languages

## Legal and Political Services

Civil Service Careers
www.civil-service-careers.gov.uk

Civil Service Fast Stream
www.faststream.gov.uk/

Legal Executives
www.cilexcareers.org.uk

Politician's Assistant
www.prospects.ac.uk/job-profiles/politicians-assistant

The Lawyer Portal
www.thelawyerportal.com

## Security and Armed Forces

British Army
www.army.mod.uk

GCHQ
www.gchq-careers.co.uk

Royal Air Force
www.raf.mod.uk

Royal Navy
www.royalnavy.mod.uk

Skills for Security
https://skillsforsecurity.org.uk

## HEALTH and SOCIAL CARE

### Healthcare

A career in Optometry
www.college-optometrists.org

A Career in Psychiatry
www.rcpsych.ac.uk/discoverpsychiatry

Careers in Podiatry
www.careersinpodiatry.com

Health Careers
www.healthcareers.nhs.uk/career-planning

How to become a Doctor
www.bma.org.uk/advice/career/

Pharmacy Careers
www.rpharms.com/resources/careers-information

Step into the NHS
www.stepintothenhs.nhs.uk

Studying for a Career in Dentistry
www.healthcareers.nhs.uk/explore-roles/dental-team

The Medic Portal
www.themedicportal.com

Thinking of becoming a Dietitian?
www.bda.uk.com/training/career/dietitians

What is Occupational Therapy?
www.rcot.co.uk

What is Physiotherapy?
www.csp.org.uk/careers-jobs

Working in Pharmaceuticals
http://careers.abpi.org.uk

Working in Public Health
www.healthcareers.nhs.uk/working-health

Want to be a Midwife?
www.rcm.org.uk/learning-and-career/

What is a Radiographer?
https://radiographycareers.co.uk

**Social Work and Counselling Services**

A Career in Counselling
www.bacp.co.uk/careers/

A Question of Care
www.aquestionofcare.org.uk

Careers in Charity
www.charityjob.co.uk/careeradvice/career-guides/

Careers in Youth Work
https://nya.org.uk/careers-youth-work/

Choosing Early Years as a Career
www.cache.org.uk/for-learners

ThinkCareCareers
www.skillsforcare.org.uk/Careers-in-care/

Want to Volunteer?
https://vinspired.com

# SCIENCE and ENVIRONMENTAL

## Building and Construction

Architectural Technicians
https://ciat.org.uk/education.html

Careers in Construction
www.citb.co.uk/careers-in-construction

Think Architecture
www.architecture.com/education-cpd-and-careers/

Women in Construction
www.goconstruct.org/construction-today/

## Engineering and Manufacturing

Born to Engineer – videos
www.borntoengineer.com/video

Careers in Aerospace
www.careersinaerospace.com/

Chemical Engineering
www.icheme.org/careers.aspx

Engineering and Technology
www.theiet.org/students/work-careers/

Motor Industry – Job Roles
www.autocity.org.uk/index.php/explore-job-roles/

Physics and Engineering
www.ipem.ac.uk/CareersJobs.aspx

Tomorrow's Engineer
www.tomorrowsengineers.org.uk

Women's Engineering
www.wes.org.uk/students

## Environment, Animals and Plants

Careers and Study Geography
www.rgs.org/geography/

Farming and Food Supply
www.brightcrop.org.uk

Geology Career Pathways
www.geolsoc.org.uk/careers

Land-Based Careers
www.lantra.co.uk/careers

## Science, Mathematics and Statistics

A Future in Chemistry
www.rsc.org/careers/future/

Becoming a Biologist
www.rsb.org.uk/careers-and-cpd/careers

Physics – Careers info and resources
www.iop.org/careers/

Science Career Pathways
www.sciencecareerpathways.com

StatsLife
www.statslife.org.uk/careers/types-of-job

# SUPPORT SERVICES

## Catering and Hospitality

Developing a Career in Hospitality
www.hospitalityguild.co.uk/A-Career-in-Hospitality/

Hospitality, Leisure and Tourism
https://careerscope.uk.net/

Tasty Careers
https://tastycareers.org.uk

## Leisure and Sport

Athletics – Get Involved
www.britishathletics.org.uk/get-involved/

Careers in Sport
https://careers-in-sport.co.uk/careers/

Horses – a career in racing
www.careersinracing.com

SkillsActive
www.skillsactive.com/sectors/our-sectors

Sport and Exercise Science
www.bases.org.uk

Sport and Leisure Management
www.prospects.ac.uk/job-profiles

Yachting, Hospitality and Watersports
https://uksa.org/professional-training/

## Personal and Other Services (Hair and Beauty)

Hair and Beauty
www.skillsactive.com/sectors/hair-beauty

Hair and Beauty Job Profiles
www.hairandbeautyjobs.com/career-hub/

General and Personal Services
https://nationalcareers.service.gov.uk/

## Retail Sales and Customer Services

Graduate Schemes
www.prospects.ac.uk/jobs-and-work-experience/

Retailing – Careers Advice
www.retailappointment.co.uk/career-advice

The Grocer
www.thegrocer.co.uk/people/

## Travel and Tourism

ABTA – Careers Info and Advice
www.abta.com/industry-zone

Hospitality, Leisure and Tourism
https://careerscope.uk.net/

Leisure Sport and Tourism
www.prospects.ac.uk/job-profiles

## Researched by Hilary Nickell

www.careercompanion.co.uk

www.ingramcontent.com/pod-product-compliance
Lightning Source LLC
LaVergne TN
LVHW012107070526
838202LV00056B/5660